JEOPARDY!®

Publications International, Ltd.

Clue and response writers: Marcus Brown and Michael R. Harris

Puzzle creators: Myles Callum and Ian Feigle

Puzzle illustrator: Kelsey Waitkus

Images from Shutterstock.com

Louis Weber, CEO
Publications International, Ltd.
8140 Lehigh Avenue
Morton Grove, Illinois 60053

ISBN: 978-1-64030-287-7

Manufactured in U.S.A.

8 7 6 5 4 3 2 1

INTRODUCTION

Jeopardy!®, "America's Favorite Quiz Show," has been challenging and educating its dedicated audience with its current version for thirty-four years. *Jeopardy!*®'s host, the well-loved Alex Trebek, has introduced a variety of categories that have redefined the vast terrain covered by general knowledge quiz shows. From light-hearted wordplay to not-well-known historical facts, the scope of *Jeopardy!*® has been able to connect with millions of people throughout the world, bringing them together under their shared pursuit of knowledge.

Brain Games®: Jeopardy! Puzzles contains a mix of sixty-seven crossword and word search puzzles based on your favorite *Jeopardy!*® categories, like Literature, World History, Potpourri, and of course, Potent Potables. And each puzzle features five *Jeopardy!*® clues straight from the writers' desks at the quiz show.

In order to complete each crossword puzzle, you will need to correctly respond to each *Jeopardy!*® clue and then deduce which of the blank crossword clues the *Jeopardy!*® response corresponds to. The correct responses will fit into the crossword space without their preceding articles (*A, An, The*), unless the article is a part of the title of a piece of art, book, movie, play, television show, etc.

In order to complete each word search puzzle, you will need to correctly respond to each *Jeopardy!*® clue and then find that response within the grid of letters. The correct responses will be found in the grid without their preceding articles (*A, An, The*), unless the article is a part of the title of a piece of art, book, movie, play, television show, etc. To finish the puzzle you will then have to find the rest of the words in the word bank. Words can be found in a straight line, horizontally, vertically, or diagonally and can be read either forward or backward.

So, there are two steps you must complete in order to solve each puzzle. First, you must correctly respond to all of the *Jeopardy!*® clues and then find them in the word search or correctly place them in the crossword. And second, you must finish finding the other words in the word search's word bank or answer the remaining crossword clues. If you ever get stuck, the answer key in the back of the book can help you. Are you ready? Grab your pencil, flip the page, and dive into the first category.

PAINTERS

1903's "THE OLD GUITARIST" IS A CLASSIC PAINTING FROM THIS SPANIARD'S "BLUE PERIOD"

WHO IS ____?

Pablo Picasso

HE BEGAN "THE ADORATION OF THE MAGI" IN 1481; THE WOMAN WITH THE SMILE CAME LATER

WHO IS ____?

Leonardo Davinci

THIS WYOMING-BORN PAINTER WAS FAMED FOR THE RADICAL "DRIP" TECHNIQUE HE USED

WHO IS ____?

Jackson Pollock

GRANT WOOD'S SISTER NAN & HIS DENTIST BYRON McKEEBY WERE THE MODELS FOR THIS 1930 PAINTING

WHAT IS ____?

American gothic

EDVARD MUNCH DID A PAINTING CALLED "THE DEATH" OF THIS MAN, BUT PLACED HIM ON A BED, NOT IN A BATH

WHO IS ____?

marat

ACROSS

1. WATERY EXPANSES
5. NEWBORN COW
9. SPANISH DIM SUM, SORT OF
14. CAME DOWN, AS ONTO A PERCH
15. "CARMEN" SHOWSTOPPER
16. NOT APPROPRIATE
17. TERHUNE'S "___ DOG"
18. GAS USED IN BRIGHT LIGHTS
19. HIGH-TECH CLASSROOM
20.
23. "LAW & ORDER: ___" (ICE-T DRAMA)
24. "THERE'S ___ HERE BUT US CHICKENS!"
25. HOOSIER PRO HOOPSTER
31. SEE FIT
32. COMMANDED, OLD-STYLE
33. CRUDE RESOURCE
36.

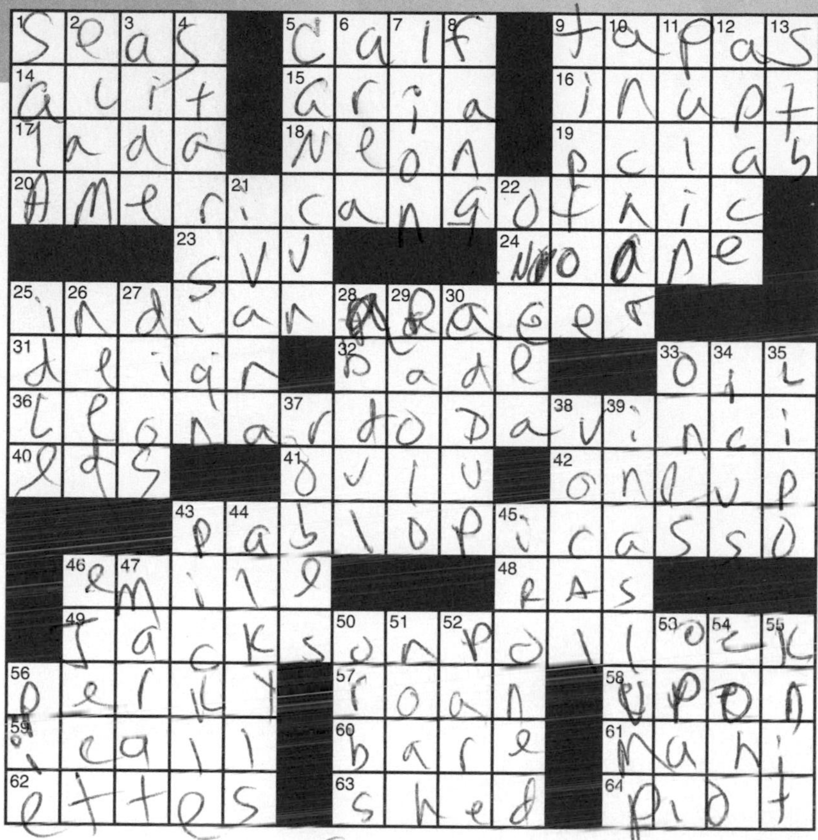

40. MAGAZINE STAFFERS, FOR SHORT
41. CITY AND CASTLE OF NORTHERN FINLAND
42. GET THE BETTER OF
43.
46. "NANA" AUTHOR ZOLA
48. DORM MONITORS, BRIEFLY
49.
56. JAUNTILY CHEERFUL
57. CHESTNUT-COLORED HORSE
58. SECOND WORD IN MANY FAIRY TALES
59. POKER PLAYER'S DECLARATION
60. DEVOID OF DUDS
61. HALF A HAWAIIAN FISH
62. "CIGAR" AND "KITCHEN" ENDINGS
63. BACKYARD STORAGE STRUCTURE
64. STORY FRAMEWORK

DOWN

1. CASA ROOM
2. ACTOR JACK OF OLD WESTERNS
3. ___-DE-CAMP
4. ARIES OR SCORPIO, E.G.
5. POPULAR YUCATAN SPRING BREAK RESORT
6. SURFACE MEASURE
7. COWARDLY OZ VISITOR
8. JACK LONDON'S "WHITE ___"
9. WALK FURTIVELY
10. COMMON NAUTICAL TATTOO
11. COMEDIAN MICHAEL OF "MONTY PYTHON"
12. SPEEDILY, TO BARDS
13. DEGREE IN RELIGION
21. A FORMER MRS. TRUMP
22. ___ MONTH (EVERY 30 DAYS OR SO)
25. DOING NOTHING
26. "ALL YOU ___ IS LOVE": BEATLES
27. GOD, IN GRANADA
28. "FOREVER YOUR GIRL" SINGER PAULA
29. FRANCESCA'S LOVE, IN DANTE'S INFERNO
30. FIND THE SUM OF
33. LOW BILLS
34. HOSP. AREAS FOR THE CRITICALLY ILL
35. FAT REMOVAL SURGERY, FOR SHORT
37. AFTER-BATH WRAPS
38. NOT SHY WITH ONE'S OPINION
39. STRUGGLING, AS A PITCHER
43. DELI DILL
44. HYDROCARBON GROUPS
45. DID A PRESSING CHORE
46. EMERGENCY FUNCTION ON A FIGHTER PLANE
47.
50. CELESTIAL SPHERES
51. BIBLE BOATWRIGHT
52. SKIN, AS AN APPLE
53. OCTOBER'S GEM
54. SALMON TYPE
55. CREATE WITH NEEDLES
56. DESSERT SERVED IN WEDGES

Answers on page 138.

STATE CAPITALS

Clue	Answer
STATE CAPITALS NAMED FOR WOMEN INCLUDE ANNAPOLIS & THIS MAINE CAPITAL	WHAT IS ____?
IT'S NICKNAMED "THE GREEN MOUNTAIN CITY"	WHAT IS ____?
IN THE OLD RAILWAY LINE IT FELL BETWEEN ATCHISON & SANTA FE	WHAT IS ____?
ONCE CALLED EDWINTON, IT WAS RENAMED FOR A GERMAN CHANCELLOR	WHAT IS ____?
THE ONLY STATE CAPITAL WHOSE NAME ENDS IN 3 VOWELS, IT'S ALSO THE NORTHERNMOST	WHAT IS ____?

ANNAPOLIS
AUSTIN
BATON ROUGE
CARSON CITY
CHEYENNE
DENVER
HELENA
JACKSON
LINCOLN
LITTLE ROCK
OLYMPIA
PIERRE
PROVIDENCE
RICHMOND
SACRAMENTO

SANTA FE

TALLAHASSEE

D	N	O	M	H	C	I	R	L	I	N	C	O	L	N
M	S	R	R	V	N	T	Z	A	Y	E	T	S	I	K
O	P	I	E	R	R	E	K	T	C	A	J	S	X	C
N	O	H	R	E	Q	E	K	N	N	B	A	F	H	O
T	L	D	B	H	P	X	E	N	I	N	C	T	E	R
P	Y	E	L	O	X	D	A	S	T	T	K	K	L	E
E	M	N	T	K	I	P	M	A	E	U	S	A	E	L
L	P	V	Q	V	O	A	F	H	V	A	O	U	N	T
I	I	E	O	L	R	E	N	E	W	E	N	G	A	T
E	A	R	I	C	H	E	Y	E	N	N	F	U	Y	I
R	P	S	K	K	B	V	K	F	K	U	R	S	L	L
B	A	T	O	N	R	O	U	G	E	J	C	T	Q	A
C	A	R	S	O	N	C	I	T	Y	A	R	A	E	P
T	A	L	L	A	H	A	S	S	E	E	B	K	U	K
K	N	X	I	U	O	T	N	E	M	A	R	C	A	S

Answers on page 138.

AFRICAN-AMERICAN HISTORY

IN THE HISTORY OF JAZZ, LOUIS ARMSTRONG WAS ONE OF THE GREATEST PLAYERS OF THIS INSTRUMENT	WHAT IS ____?
IN MONTGOMERY, ALABAMA, AFTER A YEAR-LONG BOYCOTT, INTEGRATED SEATING ON THESE BEGAN IN DEC. 1956	WHAT ARE____?
THE 1925 FILM "BODY AND SOUL" STARRED THIS POLITICAL ACTIVIST & STAGE "OTHELLO"	WHO IS ____?
ONCE CALLED "THE CAPSTONE OF NEGRO EDUCATION", THIS D.C. UNIVERSITY OPENED ITS DOORS IN 1867	WHAT IS ____?
THIS OKLAHOMA CITY'S GREENWOOD DISTRICT WAS KNOWN AS "BLACK WALL STREET" IN THE EARLY 20th CENTURY	WHAT IS ____?

ABOLITIONIST
BARACK OBAMA
CIVIL RIGHTS
COLONEL TYE
DRED SCOTT
EMANCIPATION
EQUALITY
FREDERICK DOUGLASS
FREEDMAN
FREEDWOMAN
GREAT MIGRATIONS
IDA B. WELLS
JESSE JACKSON
NAT TURNER
PRINCE HALL

REBELLIONS
RICHARD WRIGHT
SEGREGATION
TUSKEGEE

T	R	I	C	H	A	R	D	W	R	I	G	H	T	Y	H	B
U	P	R	I	N	C	E	H	A	L	L	L	W	Q	Y	V	Z
L	A	B	O	L	I	T	I	O	N	I	S	T	R	T	K	B
S	D	R	E	D	S	C	O	T	T	G	B	U	T	I	R	P
A	F	Z	E	Q	P	B	E	Y	T	L	E	N	O	L	O	C
F	R	E	D	E	R	I	C	K	D	O	U	G	L	A	S	S
X	Z	A	M	A	B	O	K	C	A	R	A	B	W	U	N	C
H	D	R	M	U	Z	R	P	H	O	W	A	R	D	Q	O	I
L	A	U	S	E	G	R	E	G	A	T	I	O	N	E	I	V
G	R	E	A	T	M	I	G	R	A	T	I	O	N	S	L	I
C	S	N	O	S	K	C	A	J	E	S	S	E	J	T	L	L
N	A	M	D	E	E	R	F	N	A	T	T	U	R	N	E	R
W	N	Z	V	T	U	S	K	E	G	E	E	U	D	Q	B	I
F	R	E	E	D	W	O	M	A	N	I	M	L	T	V	E	G
N	O	S	E	B	O	R	L	U	A	P	E	W	N	L	R	H
I	D	A	B	W	E	L	L	S	E	G	D	Q	J	T	I	T
E	M	A	N	C	I	P	A	T	I	O	N	S	B	K	X	S

Answers on page 138.

20th CENTURY WARS

IT WAS THIS CITY'S SURRENDER ON MARCH 28, 1939, THAT ENDED THE SPANISH CIVIL WAR	WHAT IS ____?
THE PERSIAN GULF WAR OF 1991 WAS FOUGHT MAINLY IN IRAQ & THIS OIL-RICH NATION NEXT DOOR	WHAT IS ____?
IN SEPTEMBER 1916 THE BRITISH ROLLED OUT THIS NEW SECRET WEAPON ON THE SOMME FRONT	WHAT IS ____?
THE INVASION OF NORMANDY INCLUDED 5 BEACHHEADS, INCLUDING THIS ONE, SECURED BY THE U.S.	WHAT IS ____?
THE KIKUYU REVOLT AGAINST WHITE SETTLERS IN 1952 KENYA WAS ALSO KNOWN AS THIS DOUBLE TALK REBELLION	WHAT IS ____?

ACROSS

1 IS OBLIGED TO
5 LEAFY ALCOVE
10
14 KRAKAUER'S "___ THE WILD"
15 CAPITAL OF IDAHO
16 SPORTS REPORTER ANDREWS
17 MOST LOYAL
19 FAIL TO PREVAIL
20 RICH DESSERT
21 X-RAY BLOCKER
23 BLANC WHO VOICED MANY A TOON
24 DOG-___ (LIKE SOME USED BOOKS)
27
29
31 BUTTE'S COUSIN
32 BOATER'S PADDLE
33 BRAZILIAN DANCE
35 COVERT GET-TOGETHER
39 JAIL FOR A SAILOR
41 HAWAIIAN COOKOUTS

43 WHAT AN ADJECTIVE MODIFIES
44 ARCTIC ICE HOUSE
46 JOHNNY CASH'S "A BOY ___ SUE"
48 COME INTO POSSESSION OF
49 SMALL NAIL
51 SPORTS CENTERS
53 HOROSCOPE DOZEN
56 POWER, SLANGILY
57 FRENCH FRIEND
58 "LITTLE ___" OF COMICS
60 EAGERLY EXPECT
64 BLANK-VERSE FOOT
66 SUPPORTER OF VICTORIA'S SECRET?
69 LARGE, THREE-TOED BIRD
70 "ALL MY CHILDREN" SIREN
71 LIKE A SNAIL OR A TURTLE
72 DOWN ___ (MAINE NICKNAME)
73 BIRD ABODES
74 GYMNASTS' GOALS

DOWN

1 "GORILLAS IN THE ___" (DIAN FOSSEY BOOK)
2 SECOND WORD OF THE GOLDEN RULE
3 DALLAS COWBOY'S EMBLEM
4 PROMOTED BOASTFULLY
5 FIRST "SHERLOCK" AIRER
6 "AWESOME!"
7 HANDLE EFFECTIVELY
8 TO BE, IN LATIN 101
9 DIRECTOR'S DO-OVER
10 BUS. CARD NUMBER
11 BAKERY WHIFF
12 AMERICAN-BORN JAPANESE
13 PREPARED TO BE DUBBED
18 COMES CLOSER
22 DO SOME LIGHT HOUSE CLEANING
25 COIN OF IRAN
26 MOUNTAINEER HILLARY
28 GIVE A HEADS-UP TO
29 ACTRESS HELGENBERGER
30 BOTANICAL SEED COVER
31
32 "MIKADO" SASH
34 SHEEP'S BLEAT
36 DOWNWARD-FACING DOG DISCIPLINE
37 TAKES TO COURT
38 BOMB LETTERS IN CARTOONS
40 ASIAN DESERT
42 LPGA STAR ___ PAK
45 TAKEN BY MOUTH
47 CAR WINDOW STICKER
50 ASTUTENESS
52 MOST RECENT
53 BELGIAN CONGO, TODAY
54
55 SMALL COINS
56 ___ DOCTOR (LAW DEGREE)
59 EUROS REPLACED THEM IN ITALY
61 READY AND WILLING
62 ELEMENT IN HEMOGLOBIN
63 FANCY MARBLES
65 CAVE-DWELLING MAMMAL
67 PLAY PART
68 ___ IN "CAT"

Answers on page 138.

AUTHORS

IN HIS "CAT'S CRADLE" FELIX HOENIKKER CREATES ICE-NINE, A SUBSTANCE THAT CAN FREEZE THE WORLD SOLID

WHO IS ____?

"SONG OF SOLOMON" WAS THE FIRST OF HER NOVELS TO HAVE A MALE PROTAGONIST

WHO IS ____?

HE BASED NORA CHARLES OF "THE THIN MAN" ON HIS FRIEND LILLIAN HELLMAN

WHO IS ____?

OAKLAND'S HEINOLD'S FIRST & LAST CHANCE SALOON WAS A FAVORITE BAR OF THIS "WHITE FANG" AUTHOR

WHO IS ____?

IT'S THE LAST NAME OF THE TWIN BROTHER AUTHORS WHO PENNED "SLEUTH" & "AMADEUS"

WHAT IS ____?

ALDOUS HUXLEY
DAVE EGGERS
DON DELILLO
GEORGE ORWELL
GEORGE SAUNDERS
JENNIFER EGAN
JHUMPA LAHIRI
JOHN BARTH
JOHN UPDIKE
JOSEPH HELLER
MARK LEYNER
PAULO COELHO
PHILIP ROTH
SAUL BELLOW
THOMAS PYNCHON

TOM WOLFE
UMBERTO ECO
URSULA K. LEGUIN
VIRGINIA WOOLF

J H U M P A L A H I R I R D F H O R T
K U R T V O N N E G U T Q X Q P H P T
S U F N V I R G I N I A W O O L F I E
U M R O S R E D N U A S E G R O E G M
I J O S E P H H E L L E R I N R E H M
E I O I U O L L I L E D N O D O U M A
H F H R Z L B U B F T O H K R W M U H
T A L R U J A I W G U C E G C J B R L
R L E O Q F T K S C N E E S E P E M L
A D O M W F Z T L Y F O R N U F R A E
B O C I P M D O P E R E N I F H T R I
N U O N M F O S V W G I N A Y J O K H
H S L O S K A T E G F U H L E K E L S
O H U T V M V L E E T S I A U O C E A
J U A U O T L E R P R R F N P Y O Y D
U X P H K W V E J A C K L O N D O N S
N L T K L A G J O H N U P D I K E E G
V E F B D A P H I L I P R O T H Z R I
T Y I F N Y D L S A U L B E L L O W I

Answers on page 139.

WOMEN WITH FLOWING TRESSES REPEAT THEM 100 TIMES A DAY; THE IMPRESSIONISTS MADE THEM VISIBLE TO THE VIEWER	WHAT ARE ____?
THIS PAINTER MARRIED DIEGO RIVERA IN 1929, DIVORCED HIM IN 1939 & MARRIED HIM AGAIN IN 1940	WHO IS ____?
THE LOUVRE'S SCULPTURE OF THIS GREEK GODDESS OF SAMOTHRACE IS ALSO CALLED "WINGED VICTORY"	WHO IS ____?
HAPPY FARMERS WERE SEEN IN THE USSR'S OFFICIAL ART, THE "SOCIALIST" TYPE OF THIS	WHAT IS ____?
USING THE LINSEED TYPE, 15th CENTURY FLEMISH PAINTERS PIONEERED THIS PAINTING SUBSTANCE	WHAT IS ____?

ACROSS

1
5 LIFT WITH A GRUNT
10 AFFIRMATIVE VOTES
14 DIVA'S SHOWPIECE
15 BURGER TOPPER
16 IT'S LEFT ON BOARD
17 SEND AGAIN
19 SHREK, FOR ONE
20 MOURNFUL BELL SOUNDS
21
23 CAESAR'S "BUT"
24 "EUREKA!"
26 NADA
27
33 KIND OF WHALE
36 GOOGLE-SEARCH RESULTS
37 FERTILITY CLINIC NEEDS
38 "LIVIN' LA VIDA ___" (RICKY MARTIN HIT)
39 FEATURES OF LIONS AND HORSES
40 DO AS DIRECTED
41 CRY OF PLEASURE

42 "PAPA" OF CLASSICAL MUSIC
43 STANDS AT THE FUNERAL
44 MUSIC FOR A SLOW MARCH
47 APHID MILKER
48 MATCHED PAIR
49 REMARKABLE TIME
52 MASS ___ (BUSES AND TRAINS)
56 FRENCH AUTHOR HUGO
58 KEPT IN CUSTODY
59
62 DATA, INFORMALLY
63 TURNED RED, MAYBE
64 CERTAIN CEREAL GRASSES
65 HEADLINER
66 ANTIQUE PHOTO TINT
67 OR ___ (THREAT WORDS)

DOWN

1 BRITISH INFORMERS
2 DANCING CASTLE
3 CASHED, AS A DOCTORED CHECK
4 COUNTESS'S MATE
5 JAPAN'S LARGEST ISLAND
6 NAVAL ACAD. GRADUATE
7 CENTER THE CROSSHAIRS
8 ___ DIRE (COURT EXAMINATION)
9 PACTS BETWEEN NATIONS
10 GOD WHO KILLED THE DRAGON PYTHON AT DELPHI
11 BASEBALL LEGEND BERRA
12 GOOFS
13 MUSHROOM STALK
18 BURGLAR DETERRENT
22 AFFECTED ATTITUDE
25 ORE APPRAISALS
27 LINGERIE BUY
28 LANGUAGE FROM WHICH "JUNGLE" AND "PUNDIT" ARE DERIVED
29 DICTATION TAKERS OF YEARS PAST
30 BIG NAME IN BEEF OR BASKETBALL
31 TILL THE COWS COME HOME
32 IMITATES SIMON
33 DINNER FROM A BUCKET
34 LIKE RICHARD OF THE ALMANAC
35 CAVERN COMEBACK
39 LARGE, POWERFUL DOGS
40
42 BARNYARD BIDDIES
43 DYE-DESIGNED FABRIC
45 FRANKNESS
46 BURNING MAN STATE
49 ANTI-KNOCK ADDITIVE
50 ROMEO AND JULIET, E.G.
51 CAME UP, IN CONVERSATION
52 THAT'S COUNTERPART
53 MUSICAL BASED ON "LA BOHEME"
54 ITALIAN CARMAKER ___ ROMEO
55 "T" ON A TEST, USUALLY
57 GIVE A HANG
60 BABYSITTER'S HANDFUL
61 LATIN GODS

Answers on page 139.

BODIES OF WATER

Clue	Response
IT'S THE WESTERNMOST & NORTHERNMOST OF THE GREAT LAKES	WHAT IS ____?
2 OF SOUTH AMERICA'S LONGEST RIVERS, THE MADEIRA & THE PURUS, FLOW INTO THIS EVEN LONGER RIVER	WHAT IS ____?
BAKU IN AZERBAIJAN & ASTRAKHAN IN RUSSIA ARE PORTS ON THIS STURGEON-FILLED SEA	WHAT IS ____?
LATVIA'S CAPITAL SHARES ITS NAME WITH THIS NEARBY GULF	WHAT IS ____?
LOCATED IN EAST-CENTRAL AFRICA, IT'S THE WORLD'S LONGEST FRESHWATER LAKE	WHAT IS ____?

BAY OF BENGAL
DANUBE
GREAT BEAR LAKE
GREAT SLAVE LAKE
GULF OF MEXICO
LAKE BAIKAL
LAKE MEADE
LAKE POWELL
LAKE TAHOE
NILE RIVER
PEYTO LAKE
PUGET SOUND
RHINE
RIVER THAMES
SEA OF JAPAN

SEINE
SNAKE RIVER
TIGRIS RIVER
YELLOW RIVER

N	A	P	A	J	F	O	A	E	S	P	R	F	Z	Z	R	M
Z	E	Q	D	B	R	I	V	E	R	T	H	A	M	E	S	F
D	N	U	O	S	T	E	G	U	P	R	H	I	N	E	A	G
L	A	K	E	T	A	N	G	A	N	Y	I	K	A	S	C	R
G	R	E	A	T	B	E	A	R	L	A	K	E	V	R	A	E
Y	R	O	I	R	E	P	U	S	E	K	A	L	D	E	U	A
E	A	L	A	K	E	P	O	W	E	L	L	A	B	V	E	T
L	E	N	I	L	E	R	I	V	E	R	N	L	M	I	L	S
L	S	G	C	N	G	P	M	B	R	U	X	W	E	R	R	L
O	N	G	E	I	K	Q	A	B	B	E	K	L	K	N	I	A
W	A	S	R	E	V	I	R	E	K	A	N	S	A	O	G	V
H	I	S	L	A	K	E	B	A	I	K	A	L	L	Z	A	E
I	P	E	O	H	A	T	E	K	A	L	H	J	O	A	G	L
V	S	I	L	A	K	E	M	E	A	D	E	R	T	M	C	A
E	A	N	F	T	L	A	G	N	E	B	F	O	Y	A	B	K
R	C	E	L	T	I	G	R	I	S	R	I	V	E	R	Y	E
O	C	I	X	E	M	F	O	F	L	U	G	I	P	M	C	B

Answers on page 139.

BUSINESS & INDUSTRY

IT'S THE BOATING TERM USED WHEN THE GOVERNMENT COMES TO THE AID OF A "SINKING" BUSINESS	WHAT IS ____?
IT WAS FORD'S FIRST CAR OFF A MOVING ASSEMBLY LINE	WHAT WAS ____?
TYPE OF WINGED BEING WHO BACKS A STARTUP VENTURE WITH MUCH-NEEDED CASH	WHAT IS ____?
8-LETTER ANATOMICAL PLURAL MEANING VISITORS VIEWING A WEBSITE	WHAT ARE ____?
PATENTED IN 1855, THE BESSEMER PROCESS DRASTICALLY LOWERED THE COST OF MAKING THIS	WHAT IS ____?

ASSOCIATION
AUTOMATION
CHARTER
COAL
CREDITORS
EMPLOYMENT
FRANCHISE
INVESTORS
MARKET
MINES
OFFSHORING
PETROLEUM
POLICY
PUBLIC
QUARRY

REGULATORS
REVENUE
SHARES

SOFTWARE
STATUTORY
UTILITIES

U Z M B T O F F S H O R I N G I V
P A U M A N Q O J T Y A Q I Y E E
L O E U A I E S X R J V L L D S Y
D A L U Y U L M E H I U G F X I Y
I W O I P Q T O Y I P A V E Y H F
M G R C C S U O U O T Q P S E C D
Y S T N I Y R T M T L I R M R N N
A J E C L N M O C A S P L T A A O
T Y P H B F I J T R T R M I W R I
L O Q A U S N W O A E I M E T F T
E Q A R P T E T T V L D O N T U A
D U V T T E S K E K L U I N O W I
O A S E P E O N Z N P N G T S P C
M R V R V L U M A R K E T E O G O
Z R A N G E L S H A R E S R R R S
Y Y I S T A T U T O R Y G I V Y S
A Z S L L A B E Y E O G M O G Q A

Answers on page 139.

COLONIAL AMERICA

THIS COLONY HAD THE FIRST PERMANENT ENGLISH SETTLEMENT	WHAT IS ____?
COINS OF THIS EUROPEAN COUNTRY WERE THOSE MOST FREQUENTLY USED IN COLONIAL AMERICA	WHAT IS ____?
DURING MUCH OF THE COLONIAL PERIOD, ITS ASSEMBLY MET ALTERNATELY AT PERTH AMBOY & BURLINGTON	WHAT IS ____?
AS PENNSYLVANIA HAD NO COAST, WILLIAM PENN WAS GIVEN LAND IN 1682 THAT LATER BECAME THIS SMALL STATE	WHAT IS ____?
BOUGHT BY THE DUTCH IN 1626, THIS ISLAND IS NAMED FOR THE INDIAN TRIBE WHO LIVED THERE	WHAT IS ____?

ACROSS

1

9 ADMIRAL BOBBY WHO DIRECTED THE NSA UNDER JIMMY CARTER

14 CARRIER WITH A MAPLE LEAF LOUNGE

15 PAPAL CAPE

16 TRICK

17 "KEMO SABE" SPEAKER

18 INITIALS OF THE "WIZARD OF MENLO PARK"

19 AGES IN HISTORY

20 BAT MAKER'S TOOL

21 CHAMPION GYMNAST KORBUT

23 PREPARE TO REMOVE, AS SNEAKERS

25 CHECK SOMEONE'S ID

27 ALLIANCE BORN IN THE COLD WAR ERA

29 AFFRONT, IN STREET SLANG

31 CELESTIAL SEASONINGS PRODUCT

■	1	2	3	4	5	6	7	8	■	9	10	11	12	13
14									■	15				
16									■	17				
18			■	19				■	20					■
21			22	■	23			24		■	25			26
■	■	■	27	28			■	29		30	■	31		
■	32	33			■	■	34				■	35		
36					■	37			■	38	39			
40			■	41	42			■	■	43				■
44			■	45			■	46	47			■	■	■
48			49	■	50		51			■	52	53	54	55
■	56			57		■	58			59	■	60		
61					■	62					63			
64					■	65								
66					■	67								■

32 BASEBALL STARTERS, IN NUMBER
34 BOTANICAL WINGS
35 ___ FRIDAY'S (RESTAURANT CHAIN)
36 ESP TEST-CARDS EPONYM
37 IT'S NOT RETURNABLE, IN TENNIS
38 COMPLETE LACK OF ORDER
40 PARROT'S CARTOON CRY
41 BRAND IN THE PET FOOD AISLE
43 BIG WEIGHTS
44 COMFY BEDWEAR
45 CONDUCTOR ___-PEKKA SALONEN
46 EYE LINER?
48 "FAMILY GUY" CREATOR MACFARLANE
50
52 SWEARING-IN WORDS
56 EARLY SYNTHETIC FIBER
58 HOLIDAY EGG DRINKS
60 SOUTH AMERICAN MONKEY
61 BLACK ___ (VERY DARK)
62 YOSEMITE'S EL CAPITAN AND OTHERS
64 CZECH TENNIS LEGEND IVAN
65 REPETITIVE PROCEDURE
66 WHAT "TWO" INDICATED, TO PAUL REVERE
67

DOWN

1 ESSENTIAL TO LIFE
2 IMPERFECT MERCHANDISE. ABBR.
3 COMPANY THAT FOUNDED NBC
4 AIRPORT BOARDING PLACE
5 DOING THE SAME OLD, SAME OLD
6 1998 OLYMPICS CITY IN JAPAN
7 "THAT IS," TO CAESAR
8 WINNIE THE POOH CREATOR'S MONOGRAM
9 SMALL BIT
10 CAMPUS ORG. FOR FUTURE ENSIGNS
11
12 JEKYLL AND HYDE, E.G.
13 PREFIX MEANING "NEW"
14 REGARDING, IN MEMOS
20 "STAR WARS" HEROINE
22 "GREEN GABLES" GIRL
24 KEEP THE ENGINE RUNNING IN PARK
26 ORATOR'S PLATFORM
28 BALD EAGLE NEST
30 OFFSHOOT GROUPS
32
33 BLOTTER BLOTCHES
34 AUG. COOLERS
36 DISPATCHES THE FLY
37 "DO I NEED TO DRAW YOU ___?"
39 ALTERNATIVE TO A TWINKIE
42 THE A IN PTA
46 BIG NAME IN TOY TRAINS
47 KIND OF GOAT OR RABBIT
49 CHRISSIE OF THE PRETENDERS
51 MAKE ___ OF (JOT DOWN)
53 UP AND ABOUT
54 CALIFORNIA-NEVADA BORDER LAKE
55 DOGPATCH POSSESSIVE
57 SOONER ST.
59 BARBECUE GO-WITH
61 TIRANA IS ITS CAP.
62 HALFWAY, FOR SHORT
63 CALL ___ DAY (QUIT WORK)

Answers on page 140.

EAST OF THE MISSISSIPPI

THE GRAND OLE OPRY MUSEUM & THE MUSIC VALLEY WAX MUSEUM ARE ATTRACTIONS IN THIS CITY	WHAT IS ____?
IN THIS ALABAMA CITY YOU CAN VISIT THE NATIONAL VOTING RIGHTS MUSEUM	WHAT IS ____?
A CONTEST FOR BLOWING CONCHS IS A HIGHLIGHT OF OLD ISLAND DAYS IN THIS FLORIDA CITY	WHAT IS ____?
THIS CITY NAMED FOR A FRENCH KING WAS FOUNDED BY GEORGE ROGERS CLARK IN 1778	WHAT IS ____?
THIS FASHIONABLE RESORT IN THE ADIRONDACKS IS THE SUMMER HOME OF THE NEW YORK CITY BALLET	WHAT IS ____?

ASHEVILLE
CHESAPEAKE BAY
CHICAGO
EAST ST. LOUIS
EVERGLADES
HATTERAS ISLAND
ILLINOIS RIVER
ISLE OF PALMS
JAMES RIVER
LAKE MENDOTA
MEMPHIS
NATCHEZ
OHIO
POTOMAC RIVER
SHENANDOAH

SMOKY MOUNTAINS

WINYAH BAY

C I A T O D N E M E K A L O H H Y

S N I A T N U O M Y K O M S I I A

S A R A T O G A S P R I N G S H I

T T K E J O N C T L K A J I L G O

E L L I V H S A N A X I H Y E Z E

E V E R G L A D E S V P Q J O V L

W I N Y A H B A Y M M O V A F Q L

D N A L S I S A R E T T A H P E I

C R E V I R S E M A J I J T A X V

D D U E I M S E L M A M O S L T E

R E V I R C A M O T O P W E M N H

C H E S A P E A K E B A Y W S A S

S H E N A N D O A H H G N Y Y T A

L O U I S V I L L E H R Y E W C B

I L L I N O I S R I V E R K H H D

D O G A C I H C M J Q R T Z X E V

E A S T S T L O U I S E N O M Z Z

Answers on page 140.

EXPLORERS

Clue	Answer
PHILIP AMADAS & ARTHUR BARLOWE EXPLORED THIS ISLAND OFF NORTH CAROLINA BEFORE ITS COLONY GOT LOST	WHAT IS ____?
IN 1773 THIS BRITISH SEA CAPTAIN CROSSED THE ANTARCTIC CIRCLE BUT NEVER SIGHTED LAND	WHO IS ____?
THIS PORTUGUESE EXPLORER COMMANDED THE FIRST FLEET TO REACH INDIA FROM EUROPE	WHO IS ____?
IN 1741 THIS DANE SIGHTED THE NORTH AMERICAN CONTINENT NEAR MOUNT ST. ELIAS, ALASKA	WHO IS ____?
FOR HIS CIRCUMNAVIGATION OF THE WORLD, HE WAS KNIGHTED ABOARD HIS GOLDEN HIND IN 1581	WHO IS ____?

ADRIAEN BLOCK
BENEDICT ALLEN
BUZZ ALDRIN
CHARLES ALBANEL
DANIEL BOONE
DIOGO CÃO
GEORGE BACK
GEORGE BASS
GERTRUDE BELL
HONG BAO
JEAN ALFONSE
KIT CARSON
LAURA BINGHAM
RICHARD E. BYRD
ROBERT BALLARD

THOMAS BUTTON
WILLIAM ADAMS

M	A	H	G	N	I	B	A	R	U	A	L	E	G	B	E	G
L	I	S	K	U	F	R	A	N	C	I	S	D	R	A	K	E
N	E	B	V	N	E	U	F	M	D	I	O	G	O	C	A	O
I	S	E	I	V	A	S	C	O	D	A	G	A	M	A	U	R
R	N	N	T	G	E	R	T	R	U	D	E	B	E	L	L	G
D	O	O	U	S	M	A	D	A	M	A	I	L	L	I	W	E
L	F	O	S	P	W	R	O	A	N	O	K	E	D	Y	E	B
A	L	B	B	R	L	L	T	O	A	B	G	N	O	H	H	A
Z	A	L	E	U	A	S	S	A	B	E	G	R	O	E	G	C
Z	N	E	R	R	I	C	H	A	R	D	E	B	Y	R	D	K
U	A	I	I	T	D	L	T	J	A	M	E	S	C	O	O	K
B	E	N	N	O	A	D	R	I	A	E	N	B	L	O	C	K
D	J	A	G	L	V	Y	Y	U	K	E	R	L	R	O	G	O
X	W	D	N	O	T	T	U	B	S	A	M	O	H	T	N	K
B	E	N	E	D	I	C	T	A	L	L	E	N	K	L	I	A
C	H	A	R	L	E	S	A	L	B	A	N	E	L	F	A	J
N	E	D	R	A	L	L	A	B	T	R	E	B	O	R	U	O

Answers on page 140.

DISCOVERIES

IN THE 1920s SCIENTISTS DISCOVERED FOSSILIZED DINOSAUR EGGS IN THIS HUGE MONGOLIAN DESERT

WHAT IS ____?

A NEW INDUSTRY IN EUROPE BEGAN IN 1747 WHEN ANDREAS MARGGRAF DISCOVERED THIS IN BEETS

WHAT IS ____?

IN 1835 JAN PURKINJE NOTED ANIMAL TISSUES, LIKE PLANT TISSUES, ARE MADE FROM THESE

WHAT ARE ____?

IN 1783 ANTOINE LAVOISIER NAMED THIS ELEMENT, FROM GREEK WORDS FOR "WATER FORMER"

WHAT IS ____?

MICHAEL FARADAY WAS AMONG THE FIRST TO FIND MAGNETISM COULD BE CONVERTED INTO THIS

WHAT IS ____?

ACROSS

1 GETS CHEEKY WITH
7 MANY A WINSLOW HOMER PAINTING
15 OPEN A PACKAGE, MAYBE
16 ALASKAN SLED RACE
17 CHESS OPENING
18 DOUBLE-CHECKED
19 NABOKOV TITLE HEROINE
20 CALL FROM A CROW
22 TIMBUKTU'S COUNTRY
23 SOFTENED IN TEMPER
26 DIDN'T CONTINUE
30 JAPANESE SLEUTH MR. ___
31 BACKING-UP SOUND
34
35 FRANK'S SPOUSE BETWEEN NANCY AND MIA
37 CAME TO REST ON A FLOWER
39 A SOLO HOMER GETS ONE
40
43 GREEK H
45 HAWAIIAN HANDOUTS

46 LEONI OF "MADAM SECRETARY"
47 GOD OF WAR
49 DECLARED
51 KEEP GOING THROUGH THE MUD
54 BROWN TONE IN OLD PHOTOS
56 BULLET BOUNCE
59 RACHEL CARSON'S SCI.
62 MILITARY VIP
63 AMTRAK STOP: ABBR.
64
68 PHYSICS PARTICLE WITH NO STRONG FORCE
70 TEXAS CITY THAT'S SPANISH FOR "YELLOW"
71 EXIT A SECURE SITE
72 FLIRT, MAYBE
73 BECOME SUDDENLY ATTENTIVE

DOWN

1
2 HEAD WREATH OF YORE
3 FRENCH WALLED CITY ON THE ENGLISH CHANNEL
4 RELIGIOUS DAY OF REST: ABBR.
5 "WAR AND PEACE," E.G.
6 ATTACKED
7 COMPUTER GAME "___ CITY"
8 ALTERNATIVE TO GOUDA
9 OPERA SET IN EQYPT
10 OLD STONE MARKER
11 SAUSAGE SKIN
12 INDONESIA'S ___ ISLANDS
13 "___ FAVOR" (SPANISH "PLEASE")
14 DUTCH PIANO CENTER
21 SPIDER'S "PARLOR"
24 AND SO ON, FOR SHORT
25 LETTER OPENER, SOMETIMES
27 BLUE FISH IN "FINDING NEMO"
28 DRAW AWAY FROM SHORE
29 502, IN OLD ROME
32 YALE PLAYER
33 EARLY BRITON
36 FLYING HOTSHOTS
38 OVERDOES IT AT THE BAR
40 "TOMBSTONE" LAWMAN
41 AUNT FROM MEXICO
42 BABY POWDER
43 PRINTER'S DASHES
44 ___ KWON DO (MARTIAL ART)
48 CALIFORNIA'S ___ NEVADA MOUNTAINS
50 ARCHAEOLOGIST'S PROJECT
52 "COME ON, THAT'S ENOUGH!"
53 "HIT THE ROAD!"
55 FLIP ___ (DECIDE BY CHANCE)
57
58 SO MUCH, IN MUSIC
60 EYEBALL IMPOLITELY
61 SIR PETER ___, PAINTER OF BRITISH ROYALTY
64 BK. BEFORE ZEPHANIAH
65 "EXOTIC" SINGER SUMAC
66 "CAN'T HELP LOVIN' ___ MAN" ("SHOW BOAT" SONG)
67 ___ VALLEY (SAN FRANCISCO NEIGHBORHOOD)
69 MICKELSON'S ORG.

Answers on page 140.

FIRST LADIES

IN 1969 SHE GRADUATED FROM WELLESLEY COLLEGE WHERE SHE WAS PRESIDENT OF THE STUDENT GOVERNMENT	WHO IS ____?
IN THE LATE 1930s, SHE TAUGHT TYPING & SHORTHAND AT WHITTIER HIGH SCHOOL IN CALIFORNIA	WHO IS ____?
IN 1992 SHE BECAME THE 1st FIRST LADY TO DELIVER A MAJOR ADDRESS AT A NATIONAL POLITICAL CONVENTION	WHO IS ____?
SHE'S BURIED IN ABILENE, KANSAS, BESIDE HER HUSBAND	WHO IS ____?
SHE WAS A HOSTESS AT THE WHITE HOUSE FOR THE WIDOWED JEFFERSON BEFORE BECOMING FIRST LADY IN 1809	WHO IS ____?

ANNA HARRISON
BETTY FORD
EDITH WILSON
ELLEN WILSON
EMILY JACKSON
HELEN TAFT
IDA MCKINLEY
JACKIE KENNEDY
JULIA TYLER
LAURA BUSH
LETITIA TYLER
MICHELLE OBAMA
NANCY REAGAN
ROSALYNN CARTER
SARAH POLK

D	O	L	L	E	Y	M	A	D	I	S	O	N	S	Q	R	X
N	P	A	R	E	T	R	A	C	N	N	Y	L	A	S	O	R
Y	C	L	C	Y	N	X	U	G	O	H	S	R	R	R	L	R
U	S	Q	H	O	L	E	P	X	O	I	B	K	A	E	A	O
B	E	L	L	E	N	W	I	L	S	O	N	X	H	W	U	C
H	F	H	E	L	E	N	T	A	F	T	N	V	P	O	R	J
D	R	O	F	Y	T	T	E	B	U	O	O	S	O	H	A	U
B	A	R	B	A	R	A	B	U	S	H	I	S	L	N	B	L
H	R	G	P	M	Q	E	J	I	J	Y	U	Q	K	E	U	I
M	A	H	D	O	R	Y	R	A	L	L	I	H	Z	S	S	A
P	N	A	N	C	Y	R	E	A	G	A	N	E	P	I	H	T
Y	F	L	E	J	A	C	K	I	E	K	E	N	N	E	D	Y
E	D	I	T	H	W	I	L	S	O	N	G	Z	M	E	F	L
L	A	M	A	B	O	E	L	L	E	H	C	I	M	I	G	E
I	A	N	O	S	K	C	A	J	Y	L	I	M	E	M	W	R
R	N	R	E	L	Y	T	A	I	T	I	T	E	L	A	K	X
A	W	Q	Y	E	L	N	I	K	C	M	A	D	I	M	Y	W

Answers on page 141.

ENDS IN "ISM"

JEAN-PAUL SARTRE WAS "THE FATHER OF" THIS MOVEMENT	WHAT IS ____?
THIS -ISM IS A GENERAL TERM FOR A VERBAL IMPROPRIETY	WHAT IS ____?
A MODERN IDEA OR INVENTION WRONGLY PLACED IN A HISTORICAL DRAMA	WHAT IS ____?
THE MYSTIC & GURU NANAK FOUNDED THIS RELIGION IN THE 1500s	WHAT IS ____?
THE PRACTICES OF SOME EXTREME PROTESTANTS OF THE REFORMATION ERA	WHAT IS ____?

ACROSS

1 ANIMAL ON PERU'S COAT OF ARMS
6 HOME OF BOGART'S FALCON?
11 "CHEERS" SETTING
14 CLASSIC COLUMN STYLE
15 BROADCAST STUDIO SIGN
16 DRINK IN A PINT
17
19 NEGATIVE DEBATE SIDE
20 HEARS A CASE AGAIN
21 EXPRESSED GRATITUDE
23 BRIGHTLY COLORED FOOD FISH
25 FLATFISH
26 HOOSIER ST.
28
33 GRAFTING SHOOT
35 ADHERENT'S SUFFIX
36 CABLE CO. BOUGHT BY AT&T IN 1999

37 VARSITY AWARDS
40 PIECE OF CAKE, PERHAPS
43 "RAVEN" INITIALS
44 "DAYS OF OUR LIVES," FOR ONE
46 CAJUN COOKERY POD
47
51 250, TO CAESAR
52 BRAND IN ROAD RUNNER CARTOONS
53
57 FORMER CHRYSLER HEAD LEE
62 BEFORE, POETICALLY
63 MANICURIST'S TOOL
65 INFLATION CAUSE?
66 THIRD HEBREW LETTER
67 GERMAN "CITY"
68 AUTHORS' OFFERINGS: ABBR.
69 END OF A STEAL, OFTEN
70 BIBLICAL PATRIARCH

DOWN

1 "PANTS ON FIRE" PERSON
2 UNESCORTED
3 ART SCH. SUBJ.
4 PINHEAD-SIZE SPY PHOTO
5 "___ OFF THE OLD BLOCK"
6 KIND OF PORK ON A CHINESE MENU
7 "RAGGEDY" GIRL
8 CAFE AU ___
9 GOMEZ ADDAMS'S PET NAME FOR HIS WIFE
10 BIG FLEET
11 THEY DISPARAGE THOSE WHO AREN'T PRESENT
12 SOOTHING BOTANICAL
13 RIP APART
18 BRING IN A HARVEST
22 BOBBSEY TWIN
24 INDIAN TERM OF RESPECT
26 ARCTIC TOOL
27 OVERLY CRITICAL SORTS
29 "___ BE A PLEASURE!" ("LOVE TO!")
30 GOLF BALL PEG
31 "BUZZ OFF!"
32 "GOOD WILL HUNTING" SCHOOL
34 YOUNG BIRDS
37 DIRECTOR SPIKE OR ANG
38 EGGS FROM THE SEA
39 "THE BRIDGE OF ___ LUIS REY"
41
42 DO PART OF A BIATHLON
45 FAMILY SCHOOL ORG.
48 GRADE OR PREP, E.G.
49 HANGER FROM AN EAVE
50 MRS. GEORGE CLOONEY
53 BASEBALL STITCHING
54 CAMERA OR EYE PART
55 BOAT'S WIND CATCHER
56 HEROINE OF "LA BOHEME"
58 VISION: PREFIX
59 IRS PROS
60 CONVEY FORMALLY
61 PAINTING, SCULPTURE, ETC.
64 BLAZED THE TRAIL

Answers on page 141.

ISLANDS

IN FRENCH POLYNESIA, THE FAAA INTERNATIONAL AIRPORT IS NEAR PAPEETE ON THIS ISLAND

WHAT IS ____?

THE PALK STRAIT SEPARATES INDIA'S TAMIL NADU STATE FROM THIS ISLAND NATION

WHAT IS ____?

THE WESTERNMOST POINT OF THIS PORTUGUESE ISLAND GROUP IS ONLY ABOUT 1,200 MILES FROM NEWFOUNDLAND

WHAT ARE ____?

THIS LARGEST JAPANESE ISLAND COVERS ABOUT 60% OF THE COUNTRY'S TOTAL AREA

WHAT IS ____?

MANILA IS ON THIS ISLAND

WHAT IS ____?

ANTIGUA
ATTU
BAFFIN
BALI
BIOKO
BIRD
BORNEO
FATIMA
IRELAND
JAVA
LONG
MAJORCA
MYKONOS
OAHU
RHODES

SAMOS
SKYE
SOCOTRA
SUMATRA
TIMOR

D	C	Q	L	N	D	N	B	O	R	N	E	O	C	Z	A	N
V	Y	X	Z	O	Z	H	H	N	N	A	V	A	J	M	E	D
F	F	C	D	Z	N	D	N	A	L	E	R	I	F	M	C	R
O	N	I	W	U	P	G	O	N	F	C	P	H	A	E	G	J
E	F	I	E	L	R	H	S	T	V	L	O	Y	T	L	A	S
S	V	S	T	O	J	B	G	I	B	I	M	P	I	N	Y	U
E	F	J	M	I	I	M	D	G	A	G	T	Y	M	I	X	Y
D	C	I	S	O	F	D	P	U	L	R	Q	I	A	F	E	Z
O	T	W	K	O	U	O	Q	A	I	U	T	E	H	F	C	U
H	J	O	S	I	X	C	U	R	I	H	A	O	Z	A	P	S
R	M	H	V	A	G	S	T	H	P	S	L	Z	C	B	T	S
Q	Y	D	Y	G	S	R	I	L	A	N	K	A	O	O	A	A
J	K	G	U	T	T	A	R	L	Z	O	R	C	A	R	S	M
E	O	D	S	U	M	A	T	R	A	H	Y	G	H	H	E	O
U	N	R	A	K	O	S	O	A	C	R	O	J	A	M	J	S
A	O	I	A	H	Y	O	Q	J	L	H	D	Y	I	X	M	C
H	S	B	L	T	J	E	W	A	Z	U	E	M	D	Y	V	T

Answers on page 141.

ENDS IN "TT"

ON APRIL 12, 1998, MARK O'MEARA SANK A 20-FOOT ONE & WON THE MASTERS GOLF TOURNAMENT BY ONE STROKE	WHAT IS ____?
THIS UNIT OF ELECTRICAL POWER IS ABBREVIATED KW	WHAT IS ____?
LAST NAME SHARED BY A FORMER SECRETARY OF THE INTERIOR & A SINCLAIR LEWIS TITLE CHARACTER	WHAT IS ____?
SYNONYM FOR A LATVIAN	WHAT IS ____?
ARMS OF THIS RHODE ISLAND BAY INCLUDE GREENWICH BAY, MOUNT HOPE BAY & THE PROVIDENCE RIVER	WHAT IS ____?

ACROSS

1 HAMILTON OF "THE TERMINATOR"
6 ABEL'S BROTHER
10 TAKES A LOAD OFF
14 BREAK OFF A RELATIONSHIP
15 QUANTITIES: ABBR.
16 PUT ___ ON (LIMIT)
17 IT'S REQUIRED TO ENTER SOME COUNTRIES
19 BARELY COOKED, AS STEAK
20 KON-___ (HEYERDAHL RAFT)
21 MEDITATION EXERCISE
22 "HAMMERIN' HANK" OF BASEBALL
23
26 SINGLE OR DOUBLE, SAY
29 LATCH ___ (ADOPT ENTHUSIASTICALLY)
30 STOP-DIME LINK
31 TENNIS BLASTS

1	2	3	4	5		6	7	8	9		10	11	12	13
14						15					16			
17					18						19			
20					21					22				
			23	24					25					
26	27	28					29							
30				31		32		33				34	35	36
37			38			39		40			41			
42				43	44		45		46	47		48		
			49			50		51			52			
53	54	55					56							
57						58					59	60	61	62
63					64					65				
66					67					68				
69					70					71				

33 MICROMANAGER'S CONCERN
37 "THE CAINE MUTINY" NOVELIST
39 DAWN'S DROPLETS
41 ___ ROMEO (ITALIAN CAR)
42 LIKE OCEAN WATER
45 CURVY SWIMMERS
48 SOME SMALL BATTERIES
49 1953 ROLE FOR LESLIE CARON
51
53 STREAKER IN THE NIGHT SKY
57 METAPHORICAL STICKING POINTS
58 BUSINESS OUTFIT
59 ___ FACTO (THEREFORE)
63 CIVIL-RIGHTS FIGURE PARKS
64 LAS VEGAS LOSER'S COMPLAINT
66 GOOD-GETS CONNECTOR
67 OTHERWISE
68 KNOT-TYING SITE
69 "AHEM" RELATIVE
70 FORMER OTTOMAN BIGWIGS
71 MUST, INFORMALLY

DOWN

1
2 CROSS INITIALS
3 BISMARCK IS ITS CAP.
4 LIKE SOME WISDOM OR INSPIRATION
5 CHOWED DOWN
6 FROLICKED
7 CLASSIC COMMODORE COMPUTER
8 "WE GOT THE OKAY!"
9 "THE PUZZLE PALACE" ORG.
10 HOME OF THE RINGLING CIRCUS MUSEUM
11 WORDS OF COMPASSION
12 FORTUNE TELLER'S CARDS
13 EXHAUSTED, AS FUNDS
18 IRA GERSHWIN CREATION
22 CARD-GAME STARTER
24 "JUST AS I THOUGHT!"
25 "WHAT'S THE REST OF THE STORY?"
26 ACKNOWLEDGES APPLAUSE
27 CELEBES OX
28 "BETTER CALL ___" ("BREAKING BAD" SPINOFF)
32 BISHOP'S DOMAIN
34 ASIAN MOUNTAIN RANGE
35 "___ FIRST YOU DON'T SUCCEED..."
36 AT THE END OF THE LINE
38
40 INTERNET LOCATIONS
43 FAULTFINDERS PICK THEM
44 "THE BOOK OF ___": DENZEL WASHINGTON FILM
46 BARISTA'S BLEND
47 AGCY. FOR NEW VENTURES
50 SHOE INSERT
52 SCOURING PAD NAME
53 FRAGMENT, AS OF PAPER
54 PEROT WHO RAN FOR PRESIDENT
55 CARAVAN PIT STOP
56 FULL OF MOXIE
60
61 "SKEDADDLE!"
62 CAJUN KITCHEN VEGGIE
64 CIVIL WAR SOLDIER, FOR SHORT
65 GRIPE ON AND ON

Answers on page 141.

LITERATURE

NABOKOV WROTE "THE GIFT" & "THE DEFENSE" IN RUSSIAN, BUT "LOLITA" IN THIS LANGUAGE	WHAT IS ____?
"THE DEAD" IS THE LAST STORY IN THIS COLLECTION BY JAMES JOYCE	WHAT IS ____?
HE CREATED DORIAN GRAY	WHO WAS ____?
THE CHARACTERS IN HEMINGWAY'S "THE SUN ALSO RISES" ALL CONVERGE TO DRINK IN THIS SPANISH CITY	WHAT IS ____?
HE WROTE "REDBURN", "OMOO", & A SEAFARING NOVEL OF SOME REPUTE	WHO IS ____?

ANTAGONIST
APOPHASIS
ASSONANCE
CONSONANCE
DYSTOPIA
EPIC
EXPOSITION
FLASHBACKS
IRONY
LEXICON
LYRICAL
METAPHOR
MYTHIC
PICARESQUE
RHYME

SARCASM
SATIRE
SIMILE
SYNECDOCHE
SYNTAX
THEORY

L D H E R M A N M E L V I L L E R
Q O H V D E H C O D C E N Y S O Q
M X A S S O N A N C E Y N A H E W
R D A O I T P O P A I O F P C D A
J T F T P L U P S O I X A A U L T
U V X O N B G A O T P T E B D I S
E B E C W Y T N I P E H L L K W I
C P U P F I S S E M S I A J F R N
N S Q I R V O F N H N E C S G A O
A A S E B P Z K R E L M I F I C G
N R E B X U M G R I O Q R X H S A
O C R E O Y J S M U E B Y H P O T
S A A R T B G I O V W L L C Z W N
N S C H C O S S T V T H E O R Y A
O M I Y N O R I P A M P L O N A A
C C P M D Y S T O P I A D R J F U
J H R E Q L T S K C A B H S A L F

Answers on page 142.

NEW YORK CITY

YOU CAN GET INTO NYC FROM NEW JERSEY BY THE LINCOLN ONE OF THESE	WHAT IS ____?
THE NAME OF THIS STREET THAT CUTS DIAGONALLY THROUGH MANHATTAN IS SYNONYMOUS WITH BIG-TIME THEATER	WHAT IS ____?
WHILE SOHO IS SOUTH OF HOUSTON STREET, THIS FASHIONABLE DISTRICT OCCUPIES A "TRIANGLE BELOW CANAL"	WHAT IS ____?
NOW NAMED FOR A BENEFACTOR, IT OPENED IN 1905 AS THE INSTITUTE OF MUSICAL ART	WHAT IS ____?
BROOKLYN WAS THE SCENE OF THE AUGUST 1776 "BATTLE OF" THIS ISLAND	WHAT IS ____?

BATTERY PARK
BOWERY
BRONX
BROOKLYN
CENTRAL PARK
CHELSEA
COBBLE HILL
COLLEGE POINT
FDR DRIVE
FLATBUSH
FLUSHING
HARLEM
HARLEM RIVER
HART ISLAND
HELL'S KITCHEN

PARK AVE
PROSPECT PARK
QUEENS
RIKERS ISLAND
UPTOWN

L	B	A	T	T	E	R	Y	P	A	R	K	Q	X	H	X	U
T	R	A	C	Q	R	E	V	I	R	M	E	L	R	A	H	K
N	O	E	A	E	D	V	E	B	P	O	Q	O	E	E	F	R
I	O	S	U	P	B	N	L	V	Y	B	J	D	L	B	L	A
O	K	L	L	N	D	I	A	E	A	M	Q	L	G	O	U	P
P	L	E	K	L	Y	N	R	L	N	K	S	U	N	C	S	T
E	Y	H	R	X	I	H	A	T	S	K	R	G	E	F	H	C
G	N	C	A	S	A	H	H	L	I	I	I	A	D	E	I	E
E	J	L	P	R	U	S	E	T	S	S	S	R	P	I	N	P
L	G	U	L	K	D	N	C	L	L	I	D	R	J	D	G	S
L	U	E	A	J	N	H	Y	A	B	R	T	U	E	D	P	O
O	M	P	R	U	E	O	N	R	I	B	L	R	I	K	A	R
C	O	O	T	N	W	D	E	V	E	L	O	N	A	R	I	P
R	N	X	N	O	R	B	E	Z	I	W	T	C	H	H	S	R
V	C	P	E	K	W	A	P	A	G	B	O	S	M	S	C	X
D	C	I	C	X	D	N	R	F	L	A	T	B	U	S	H	W
Q	U	B	R	O	A	D	W	A	Y	X	G	J	S	N	W	L

Answers on page 142.

MUSIC

MICK JAGGER SINGS BACKUP ON HER HIT "YOU'RE SO VAIN"

WHO IS ____?

THIS N.E.R.D SINGER HAS A 24 HOUR MUSIC VIDEO FOR HIS SONG "HAPPY"

WHO IS ____?

HER "PEARL" ALBUM WASN'T YET COMPLETED WHEN SHE DIED IN 1970

WHO IS ____?

FROM 1969, IT'S THE MUSICAL TALE OF A "DEAF, DUMB & BLIND KID" WHO "SURE PLAYS A MEAN PINBALL"

WHAT IS ____?

THIS RAPPER SOUGHT THE HELP OF CONTEMPORARY JAZZ ARTISTS FOR HIS ALBUM "TO PIMP A BUTTERFLY"

WHO IS ____?

ACROSS

1 "THE PRISONER OF ___" (FAIRBANKS FILM)
6 APHRODITE'S BEAU
10 MISHAPS FOR QBS
14 FUGARD'S "A LESSON FROM ___"
15 EPIC CHRONICLE
16 GERMAN "NINE"
17
19 BITE-SIZE APPETIZER
20 ESPIONAGE DOUBLE AGENTS
21 MORE TIGHTLY DRAWN
23 SPEEDING ALONG
25
27 "WATER MUSIC" COMPOSER NED
28 NON-PRO SPORTS ORG.
29 GET UNDER ONE'S SKIN
30 NON-PRO SPORTS ORG.
31 STABLE HAND OF YORE

33
38 NOT EXACTLY A THRILL
39 OLD OFFICE NOTE-TAKERS
41 BOTANIST'S FIELD
45 ASTRONAUT GRISSOM
47 EUR. DEFENSE ASSN.
48
52 SAILOR, SLANGILY
53 HOW FREELANCE WORK IS OFTEN DONE
54 "THE FAULT, DEAR BRUTUS, IS NOT ___ STARS"
56 GIVE A GRADE TO
57 TIME PERIOD THAT COVERS THE LAST FEW WEEKS, SAY
62 FOSSEY IN "GORILLAS IN THE MIST"
63 DOESN'T LAST FOREVER
64
65 BALTIC STATES, ONCE: ABBR.
66 MAE OR NATHANAEL
67 FOLLOW AS A CONSEQUENCE

DOWN

1 EFRON OF "HIGH SCHOOL MUSICAL"
2 OLD MUSIC NOTE (OR A DRINK BACKWARDS)
3 OSCAR WINNING SALLY FIELD ROLE
4 1980S AUTO WITH GULL-WING DOORS
5 PLACE OF REFUGE
6 "NO RETURNS ON THIS ITEM"
7 ARIES' ANIMAL
8 DIVA'S PROBLEM
9 CHRISTMAS DROP-IN?
10 HOW BOARD GAME PLAYERS PLAY
11 STRAIGHTEN UP
12 ELVIS'S MISSISSIPPI BIRTHPLACE
13 ALL TANGLED UP
18 CAPITOL HILL VIP
22 BIBLICAL LANDFALL LOCATION
23 "PRINCE VALIANT" SON
24 ONE OF TWO METRONOME SOUNDS
25 FIX HASTILY AND TEMPORARILY
26 BRUCE BANNER'S ALTER EGO, WITH "THE"
28 CRUMBLY ITALIAN CHEESE
31 NBA'S MAGIC, ON SCOREBOARDS
32 GOLF STAR ERNIE
34 EARLY DATA STORAGE SOFTWARE
35 PIECES ON CHESSBOARDS
36 LEMON AND MELON, E.G.
37 FORMER NEWSPAPER SECTION FOR SHORT
40 CRY NOISILY
41 NORWEGIAN COAST FEATURES
42 POLYNESIAN PORCHES
43 AUTO SAFETY/TRACKING SYSTEM
44 MATURES ON THE VINE
46 MOST CRAFTY
49 EDDIE BAUER RIVAL
50 HOMEY HOSTEL
51 "BUONA ___" (ITALIAN SIGN-OFF)
55 BRUSH ___ (REVIEW)
58 COMPASS DIR. NEAR 2 O'CLOCK
59 AUDIOPHILE'S COLLECTION
60 CHURCH-FOUNDED DALLAS SCH.
61 ROPE ON A SHIP

Answers on page 142.

POETS AND POETRY

POE POEM CONTAINING THE LINE "WHAT A WORLD OF HAPPINESS THEIR HARMONY FORETELLS!"	WHAT IS ____?
AMONG THE WRITERS IN THIS MOVEMENT, BYRON IS MORE HIGHLY ESTEEMED THAN DARLEY	WHAT IS ____?
ONLY 7 OF HER 1,775 POEMS WERE PUBLISHED DURING HER LIFETIME	WHO IS ____?
SHE'S WON 2 GRAMMYS FOR ALBUMS OF HER POETRY, "ON THE PULSE OF MORNING" & "PHENOMENAL WOMAN"	WHO IS ____?
PETRARCH'S "CANZONIERE" INCLUDED 366 SONNETS, ONE A DAY, TO THIS LADY WITH WHOM HE WAS INFATUATED	WHO IS ____?

ALLEGORY
ALLUSION
BLANK VERSE
CESURA
COUPLET

E.E. CUMMINGS
ELEGY
END-STOP
EPIGRAPH
GHAZAL

JOHN ASHBERRY
METER
PABLO NERUDA
PROSODY
REFRAIN

RUMI	STANZA	VERSE
SHARON OLDS	SYLVIA PLATH	VERSIFICATION
SONNET	TRIPLET	VILLANELLE

D	F	V	A	A	Z	N	A	T	S	C	O	U	P	L	E	T
L	P	J	R	M	A	Y	A	A	N	G	E	L	O	U	I	L
W	J	H	U	N	Y	R	R	E	B	H	S	A	N	H	O	J
P	R	O	S	O	D	Y	B	L	A	N	K	V	E	R	S	E
N	S	A	E	M	I	L	Y	D	I	C	K	I	N	S	O	N
J	I	L	C	V	I	L	L	A	N	E	L	L	E	I	N	I
W	L	A	Z	A	H	G	T	H	E	B	E	L	L	S	M	X
S	H	A	R	O	N	O	L	D	S	R	W	B	L	U	N	L
E	T	S	P	F	X	P	A	B	L	O	N	E	R	U	D	A
E	O	D	K	T	E	L	P	I	R	T	G	M	K	F	H	U
S	O	N	N	E	T	R	P	O	T	S	D	N	E	P	X	R
E	L	E	E	C	U	M	M	I	N	G	S	E	A	T	N	A
L	E	N	O	I	T	A	C	I	F	I	S	R	E	V	E	O
E	N	S	Q	G	N	G	V	Y	R	O	G	E	L	L	A	R
G	W	I	R	T	R	S	Y	L	V	I	A	P	L	A	T	H
Y	D	D	I	E	H	Z	A	L	P	Q	U	L	B	E	G	O
O	R	C	A	W	V	M	A	E	A	L	L	U	S	I	O	N

Answers on page 143.

MYTHOLOGY

IN JAPANESE MYTHOLOGY, INARI IS THE GOD OF THIS GRAIN	WHAT IS ____?
IN AN AFRICAN MYTH, ANANSI, A TRICKSTER IN THE FORM OF THIS, TRAVELS THE WORLD ON HIS WEB STRINGS	WHAT IS ____?
SOME JEWISH LEGENDS PORTRAY THIS MONSTER, WHOSE NAME MEANS "UNFORMED", AS A DEFENDER OF THE JEWS	WHAT IS ____?
HEIMDALL GUARDED THE BIFROST RAINBOW BRIDGE LEADING TO THIS REALM, THE HOME OF VALHALLA	WHAT IS ____?
IN GREEK MYTH THE WHIRLPOOL CHARYBDIS LAY OPPOSITE THIS SEA MONSTER WITH 6 DOGS' HEADS	WHAT IS ____?

ACROSS

1 NICKNAME OF TV'S TEMPERANCE BRENNAN
6 LOOK OVER HASTILY
10 BRIDGE LENGTH
14 CRUSOE, BEFORE FRIDAY
15 JIMMY OF SHOES
16 BIG NAME IN THE DETERGENT AISLE
17 YARN-HAIRED REDHEAD
19 MOHAMMED ___ PAHLAVI (FORMER SHAH OF IRAN)
20 THE "S" IN GPS, BRIEFLY
21 MENU TERM WITH TUNA OR PATTY
22
24 FISHING-ROD ATTACHMENT
25 1986 BOOK BY ROCKER TURNER
26 FORMER FUJI COMPETITOR
29 MARMALADE-LOVING BEAR

33 THEY HAVE SHUTTLES AND TREADLES
35
36 SCREWBALL COMEDIAN PHILIPS
37 ACTOR GULAGER OF OLD TV WESTERNS
38 SECOND-RATE BOXER
41 CIVIL WAR SOLDIER, FOR SHORT
42 ON TOP OF, POETICALLY
43 GOT ___ RAP: WAS FALSELY ACCUSED
44 ROOMY SIZE
46 MISSING-CHILD BULLETIN
50 LIKE PINOCCHIO, EVENTUALLY
51 "I DON'T NEED ___" (RESTAURANT REGULAR'S COMMENT)
52 PARTY THROWING A PARTY
54
56 COLOR ON A WINDSHIELD
57 FASHION'S BOTTOM LINE?
60 KINGS FROM THE EAST
61 SUNKIST PRODUCT
64 FIRST-YEAR LAW STUDENT
65 "FIDDLER" OF OLD ROME
66 APARTMENT VACANCY SIGN
67 SUN. ORATIONS
68 DRAINS STRENGTH FROM
69 GRACEFUL PADDLERS

DOWN

1 HAPPY HOUR SITES
2 NEUTROGENA RIVAL
3 RICH YULETIDE QUAFFS
4 MIT GRAD, OFTEN
5 DREADED TEACHER'S NOTE
6
7 INFORMAL CONVERSATION
8 GET AN ___ (ACE, AS A TEST)
9 LIKE TEFLON-TREATED PANS
10 CAT'S-CRADLE NEED
11 APARTMENT FOR TRIPS TO THE CITY
12 AXELIKE TOOL
13 JUST STEPS AWAY
18 LIKE ONE END OF A POOL
23 GLAND THAT PRODUCES MELATONIN
24 HIT HEADFIRST
25 PREFIX MEANING "PERSONAL"
26 BIG NAME IN ALUMINUM
27
28 HOMER
30 SUFFIX WITH AIR OR HIPPO
31 GREEK ALPHABET ENDING
32 SWEDE WHO HAD 350 PATENTS
34 LESS BOUNTIFUL
39 LEAVES HIGH AND DRY
40 SHE SANG "TO SIR WITH LOVE"
45 ETCHINGS, PAINTINGS, ETC.
47 COMMUNICATES ONLINE
48 HORNED HERBIVORES
49 CHINESE SECRET SOCIETY
53 LETS STAND, EDITORIALLY
54 "FAMOUS" COOKIE PIONEER
55 OF SOUND MIND
56 BALLFIELD COVERING
57 HAVANA HI
58 GENESIS LOCATION
59 YOGA CLASS PADS
62 STEPHEN OF "THE CRYING GAME"
63 DO A SEEDY JOB?

Answers on page 143.

POTENT POTABLES

A MIMOSA IS EQUAL PARTS ORANGE JUICE & THIS POTENT POTABLE	WHAT IS ____?
A BESTSELLING IMPORTED LIQUEUR IN THE U.S. IS THIS COFFEE-FLAVORED ONE FROM MEXICO	WHAT IS ____?
IF YOU USE VODKA INSTEAD OF RUM IN THIS PINEAPPLE COCKTAIL IT'S CALLED A CHI CHI	WHAT IS ____?
THIS FERMENTED HONEY-&-WATER BEVERAGE WAS A FAVORITE OF CHAUCER'S MILLER & BEOWULF	WHAT IS ____?
THE POPULAR LIQUEUR KNOWN AS "SLOE" THIS IS MADE FROM THE FRUIT OF THE BLACKTHORN	WHAT IS ____?

AVIATION
BARLEY
BEER
BITTERS
BRANDY
CURACAO
DAIQUIRI
DRAUGHT
FERMENT
LAGER
MAI-TAI
MERLOT
MEZCAL
NEGRONI
OUZO

PORTER
SAISON
SAKE
SNIFTER
SOJU
STOUT

P Q F B W K G D N N M R J N R R V
O K I U A K P H Z A A N I Z O E F
R Y N W S W I F L N U G H V X T K
T I O B C B N Q N O U S Z D V F G
E R R O N R A V I A T I O N F I G
R I G E T W C S F L S H Z Y E N J
E U E W H F O C R A R W U D R S Z
Z Q N E G J L D H C E X O N M E X
Z I K Q U O A B K Z T I A A E N B
K A F N A V D A C E T M P R N G K
S D Q C R X A R X M I J K B T A Q
I E A U D U N L Y B B J U A H P M
D H B R X Q O E J O E N F L U M E
L Z C A E M S Y M Y J E U G S A R
P Q G C C Z I E R M U A R A A H L
R E G A L M A I T A I U Q C A C O
O G A O Z D S A U Q Y V S T O U T

Answers on page 143.

POTPOURRI

LINCOLN'S PORTRAIT ON THE U.S. $5 BILL IS FROM A PHOTOGRAPH TAKEN AT THIS MAN'S STUDIO	WHO IS ____?
MISS PIGGY KNOWS THIS MUPPETEER'S ORIGINAL LAST NAME WAS OZNOWICZ	WHO IS ____?
IN THIS SPORT A LONG BASKET CALLED A CESTA IS WORN ON ONE HAND	WHAT IS ____?
ON THIS SITCOM CHICAGO COP CARL WINSLOW'S PET PEEVE WAS HIS NEIGHBOR STEVE	WHAT IS ____?
THESE BIVALVES ARE THE MAIN INGREDIENT IN THE FRENCH DISH MOULES MARINIERE	WHAT ARE ____?

ARABLE
ASIAN
ASPIC
BENTHIC
BIFURCATION
CONFESSION
CYBERPUNK
DESKTOP
DRACONIAN
DRONES
FARMHAND
IDEOLOGY
MAINE COON
METADATA
MYCELIUM

NEOCORTEX
QUICKSAND
REALIST
SAUTEE
SKEPTIC
SPIRITUAL
VALLEY

O S Y S S Y M A I N E C O O N A X
D A D E Y G O L O E D I D F F S O
Q T S I L A E R T E L B A R A A B
Y U W V P L C U S L C M S L H W N
D M I S F P A K L I I L P A N O E
A U N C O S T V H L E X R U I U O
R I A I K O D T Y S K E P T I C C
B L I P P S N M S D M R A I C I O
W E N S H E A U T D N C P R W A R
E C O A B T M N N F R Y S I W L T
H Y C C T W F A D U A O T P H A E
T M A E D H I R F I V R N S Z I X
A P R S B S P I A G C H M E Q A O
M S D V A G B W O N Q L H H S J Q
A T A D A T E M O X K H Y K A D M
C O N F E S S I O N A O U L B N Z
C Y B E R P U N K B J T Z Z P F D

Answers on page 144.

RIVERS

ON ITS TRIP THROUGH EGYPT, THIS RIVER HAS NO TRIBUTARIES

WHAT IS ____?

WHILE ROWING DOWN THIS RIVER, YOU'LL PASS OXFORD UNIVERSITY & WINDSOR CASTLE

WHAT IS ____?

THE MAIN DRAIN OF NORTHERN ITALY, ITS DELTA AT THE ADRIATIC SEA HAS NUMEROUS MOUTHS

WHAT IS ____?

THIS RIVER FEATURED ON THE STATE FLAG OF NEBRASKA BEARS THE NAME OF ANOTHER STATE

WHAT IS ____?

IN 1960 INDIA & PAKISTAN SIGNED A TREATY TO DEAL WITH CONTROL OF THE WATERS OF THIS RIVER

WHAT IS ____?

ACROSS

1 APT RHYME OF "AAHS"
5 "NEVER CRY WOLF" AUTHOR FARLEY
10 DO LAPS IN THE POOL
14 BOUNCY TUNE
15 WORDS AT A WELL
16 "SAY IT ISN'T SO!"
17 OLD FORM OF ITALIAN MUSICAL DRAMA
19 AUCTION OFFERS
20 ATTACKS FROM ALL SIDES
21 AUSTEN HEROINE
23 ONE OF SEVEN ABBRS. ON A CALENDAR
24 SEEMING ETERNITIES
26 MORE THAN NEEDED
28 DEMONSTRATE THAT YOU'RE UP TO DATE?
30 FROM LAOS OR TIBET, E.G.
31

1	2	3	4	■	5	6	7	8	9	■	10	11	12	13
14				■	15					■	16			
17				18						■	19			
20						■	21			22	■	23		
■	■	■	24			25		■	26		27			
■	28	29					■	30					■	■
■	31		■	32			33		■	34			35	36
37			38	■	39				40	■	41			
42				43	■	44				45	■	46		
■	■	47			48		■	49			50			■
51	52					■	53					■	■	■
54			■	55		56		■	57			58	59	60
61			62	■	63			64						
65				■	66					■	67			
68				■	69					■	70			

32 LESS CONSTRAINED
34 SITE FOR MOGULS
37 AXE HANDLE
39 CARIBBEAN CRUISE STOPS
41 ACTOR HEMSWORTH
42 "CROCODILE ROCK" SINGER JOHN
44 EVERY BOOK HAS ONE
46 COUSINS OF AVES
47 PROSPEROUS PERIODS
49 SUDDEN SILENCES
51 EGYPTIAN SUN GOD
53 CUM LAUDE MODIFIER
54 MOO GOO ___ PAN (CHINESE DISH)
55 SILENT CLOWN
57 FENCING PLOYS
61
63 "MMM, YUM!"
65 U.S. DEPT. WITH A WINDMILL ON ITS SEAL
66 DIARIST NIN
67 WORDS BEFORE SNAG OR HOMER
68 JOINS IN MATRIMONY
69 ALASKA OR HAWAII, OFTEN, ON MAPS
70 HARDLY A WALK IN THE PARK

DOWN

1 NEATNIK'S NIGHTMARE
2 ACCESSORY FOR SHERLOCK HOLMES
3 BREWPUB ARRAY
4 SIGN OF A BAD WINDOW WASHER
5
6 HAVE DEBTS
7 MESS BEHIND A COMPUTER
8 BARRY MANILOW'S "AS SURE ___ STANDIN' HERE"
9
10 REACT TO A TEARJERKER
11 RECORDING OF RAIN, MAYBE
12
13 GRANDMA OF ART
18 DINED ON, BIBLICALLY
22 CENTER OF ROTATION
25 BIG BLASTS FROM THE PAST, BRIEFLY
27 WORD WITH CURTAIN OR CATTLE
28 "BE ___!" ("HELP ME OUT HERE!")
29 EGG ORDER
30 "QUEEN OF SOUL" FRANKLIN
33 YALE ROOTER
35 NEW ENGLAND TEAM, FOR SHORT
36 SOME PRINTING DASHES
37 AT. NO. 2'S SYMBOL
38 GOOFY OR DAFFY, E.G.
40 THRILLA IN MANILA, E.G.
43 "CHEERS" REGULAR
45 ANGLO-SAXON SLAVES
48 COCKTAIL CREATED AT TRADER VIC'S
50 OLD SAN FRANCISCO HIPPIE HANGOUT, WITH "THE"
51 VICE PRESIDENT WHO RESIGNED IN 1973
52 BAR HARBOR'S STATE
53 BADLANDS PLATEAUS
56 "BUDDENBROOKS" AUTHOR
58 BLACK, AT THE ROULETTE TABLE
59 BAG FOR SHOPPING
60 MOUNT RUSHMORE'S ST.
62 HECTIC HOSP. SECTIONS
64 GIFT IN A LONG, THIN BOX

Answers on page 144.

U.S. PRESIDENTS

BEFORE HE WAS PRESIDENT, HE LIVED THE LIFE OF A COWBOY ON HIS NORTH DAKOTA RANCH	WHO IS ____?
DURING HIS TERM, THE VOTING AGE WAS LOWERED FROM 21 TO 18	WHO IS ____?
BILL CLINTON'S MIDDLE NAME, IT'S ALSO THE LAST NAME OF ANOTHER PRESIDENT	WHAT IS ____?
IN MAY 1846, 14 MONTHS AFTER POLK TOOK OFFICE, THE U.S. DECLARED WAR ON THIS COUNTRY	WHAT IS ____?
THE WHITE HOUSE WAS BURNED BY THE BRITISH WHILE HE WAS PRESIDENT	WHO IS ____?

COMMANDER IN CHIEF
DIPLOMACY
ELECTED
ELECTION DAY
FEDERALIST
FOREIGN POLICY
GERALD FORD
HERBERT HOOVER
IMPEACHED
INAUGURATION
JIMMY CARTER
NATIONAL UNION
PARDON
RONALD REAGAN
SUCCESSION

VETO
VICE PRESIDENT
WHIG

D	E	T	C	E	L	E	C	X	I	G	J	X	W	H	I	G
I	N	A	U	G	U	R	A	T	I	O	N	S	Z	Z	M	Q
N	V	Q	Y	U	G	E	R	A	L	D	F	O	R	D	P	N
O	N	O	X	I	N	D	R	A	H	C	I	R	R	F	E	V
S	P	F	I	N	O	I	N	U	L	A	N	O	I	T	A	N
R	T	E	D	D	Y	R	O	O	S	E	V	E	L	T	C	H
E	G	D	S	Y	A	D	N	O	I	T	C	E	L	E	H	J
F	R	E	V	O	O	H	T	R	E	B	R	E	H	N	E	I
F	B	R	I	W	J	F	R	K	J	Y	N	Q	F	G	D	M
E	P	A	R	D	O	N	D	I	P	L	O	M	A	C	Y	M
J	M	L	R	O	N	A	L	D	R	E	A	G	A	N	Y	Y
U	L	I	U	H	O	C	I	X	E	M	Y	V	O	Z	X	C
U	M	S	S	U	C	C	E	S	S	I	O	N	T	M	A	A
Z	I	T	V	I	C	E	P	R	E	S	I	D	E	N	T	R
F	O	R	E	I	G	N	P	O	L	I	C	Y	V	X	N	T
C	O	M	M	A	N	D	E	R	I	N	C	H	I	E	F	E
N	O	S	I	D	A	M	S	E	M	A	J	P	P	V	J	R

Answers on page 144.

SCIENCE

MARBLE IS CLASSIFIED AS A METAMORPHIC ROCK; BEFORE THAT IT WAS LIMESTONE, THIS TYPE OF ROCK

WHAT IS ____?

SEED PLANTS ARE DIVIDED INTO 2 MAIN GROUPS: ANGIOSPERMS & THESE, WHICH INCLUDE THE CONIFERS

WHAT ARE ____?

ONE ESTIMATE SAYS THERE ARE ABOUT 326 MILLION CUBIC MILES OF THIS COMPOUND IN, ON & ABOVE THE EARTH

WHAT IS ____?

THIS "PREFRONTAL" MEDICAL PROCEDURE INVOLVES THE DESTRUCTION OF SECTIONS OF THE BRAIN'S CORTEX

WHAT IS ____?

THE PROCESS BY WHICH NEUTRAL ATOMS BECOME ELECTRICALLY CHARGED IS CALLED THIS

WHAT IS ____?

ACROSS

1 DINER SIGN
5 QUANTITY OF GRAIN OR ARROWS
10 TAKES A CHAIR
14 ACTRESS SORVINO
15 "A CONFEDERACY OF DUNCES" AUTHOR
16 OPERA HIGHLIGHT
17 ANY BEATLE, ONCE
18
20 POPULAR ONLINE LECTURES ABOUT "IDEAS WORTH SPREADING"
22 "SIDDHARTHA" NOVELIST
23 DOMED HOME: VAR.
24 ART COLONY NEAR SANTA FE
26
30 VANNA'S COHOST
33 EQUIPPED, AS A ROWBOAT
34 OPPOSITE OF MESSY
35 REGRET

36 ELECTRICAL RESISTANCE UNITS
37 COTTON-CANDY HOLDERS
39 PET-SHOP PURCHASE
40 ROCK BAND ___ FIGHTERS
41 RIGHTS GROUP, FOR SHORT
42 POET WYSTAN HUGH
43 ___ KIPPUR (JEWISH HOLIDAY)
44
47 COVERS WITH TURF
48 ATLANTA'S ARENA, ONCE
49
52
56 ALL POLITICS, TO WILL ROGERS
59 ARCH WITH A DOUBLE-S SHAPE
60 "AH, OK"
61 AMERICAN FUR COMPANY FOUNDER
62 ___ BATOR (CAPITAL OF MONGOLIA)
63 G-MEN AND THE LIKE
64 WHISTLES OF RELIEF
65 GYMNASTS' PERFECT SCORES

DOWN

1 GIVE OFF, AS LIGHT
2 APTLY NAMED ASSISTANT
3 DID NOT STEP LIGHTLY
4 CHOWDER GO-WITH
5 MOONSHINE MACHINES
6 CONNECT, AS A STEREO
7 UNFATHOMABLE STRETCHES
8 BOXER WHO WON THE THRILLA IN MANILA
9 CASABLANCA HEADGEAR
10 FILLS AND THEN SOME
11 PIGMENTED EYE PART
12 PADRE'S BROTHERS
13 ENTIRELY SENSIBLE
19 "___ OF GOLDEN DAFFODILS": WORDSWORTH
21 STEINBECK'S "TO ___ UNKNOWN"
24 BAOBAB OR ACACIA
25 AMO, ___, AMAT
26 DISNEY CHARACTER ORIGINALLY NAMED DIPPY DAWG
27 BRUTE IN "GULLIVER'S TRAVELS"
28 1983 COMEDY WITH THE LINE "KENNY, DON'T PAINT YOUR SISTER!"
29 THAT BORED FEELING
30 "THE DEVIL WEARS ___"
31 HOLE-MAKING TOOL
32 RELATIVE OF ITTY-BITTY
37 INCL. ON THE DISTRIBUTION LIST
38 CUTLASS OR 88, INFORMALLY
39 "STOP THAT!"
41 STICK OUT LIKE ___ THUMB
42 THE A OF A.D.
45 MILKED ANIMAL, IN KIDDIE-SPEAK
46 CAMPFIRE LEFTOVERS
47 TENNIS CHAMP MONICA
49 COSETTE, E.G., IN "LES MISERABLES"
50 ALTAR END OF A CHURCH
51 FESTOONED WITH BATHROOM TISSUE, INFORMALLY
52 STRINGS FOR A MINSTREL
53 EYEBALL RUDELY
54 LIKE MR. MUSTARD
55 LONGS (FOR)
57 CARPENTER'S CUTTER
58 BURNT RESIDUE

Answers on page 145.

U.S. HISTORY

MERIWETHER LEWIS SERVED AS THE MIDWIFE WHEN HER SON JEAN BAPTISTE WAS BORN ON FEBRUARY 11, 1805	WHO IS ____?
ON MARCH 1, 1803, IT BECAME THE FIRST STATE CREATED OUT OF THE NORTHWEST TERRITORY	WHAT IS ____?
ABOUT 4,000 CHEROKEE INDIANS DIED ON THE "TRAIL OF" THESE IN THE LATE 1830s	WHAT ARE ____?
NICKNAME OF THE AREA ABANDONED BY FOLKS IN THE 1930s TO GO TO CALIFORNIA	WHAT IS ____?
PRES. HARDING'S INTERIOR SECRETARY ALBERT FALL SPENT 9 MONTHS IN PRISON FOR HIS ROLE IN THIS SCANDAL	WHAT IS ____?

ABOLITIONISM
BAY OF PIGS
BULL RUN
CHAHOKIA
CIA
CIVIL WAR
COLD WAR
FBI
FORT SUMTER
GOLD RUSH
IMPERIALISM
JAMESTOWN
KIT CARSON
LABOR MOVEMENT
LEMHI PASS

MUCKRAKER
NEW DEAL
PEARL HARBOR
PENTAGON
PROGRESSIVISM
PROHIBITION
SANTA FE TRAIL
SEMINOLE WARS

N	L	E	M	H	I	P	A	S	S	G	S	F	A	R	K	J
U	B	K	C	L	A	B	O	R	M	O	V	E	M	E	N	T
V	U	S	A	N	T	A	F	E	T	R	A	I	L	T	H	R
S	R	A	E	T	B	A	Y	O	F	P	I	G	S	M	M	E
S	A	C	A	J	A	W	E	A	G	O	L	D	R	U	S	H
R	O	X	C	O	L	D	W	A	R	B	U	T	I	S	I	S
A	P	R	O	G	R	E	S	S	I	V	I	S	M	T	N	E
W	N	J	A	M	E	S	T	O	W	N	W	U	U	R	O	L
E	O	P	F	G	I	R	A	W	L	I	V	I	C	O	I	H
L	G	S	J	N	O	S	R	A	C	T	I	K	K	F	T	U
O	A	B	U	L	L	R	U	N	H	P	U	J	R	F	I	L
N	T	E	M	O	D	T	O	P	A	E	T	M	A	U	L	A
I	N	N	O	I	T	I	B	I	H	O	R	P	K	H	O	E
M	E	R	E	D	U	S	T	B	O	W	L	O	E	I	B	D
E	P	I	V	S	Z	N	T	S	K	E	P	C	R	O	A	W
S	I	M	P	E	R	I	A	L	I	S	M	X	I	M	O	E
K	I	F	P	E	A	R	L	H	A	R	B	O	R	A	I	N

Answers on page 145.

WEST OF THE MISSISSIPPI

THIS STATE HAS STATE PARKS NAMED FOR CURT GOWDY NEAR BUFORD & BUFFALO BILL NEAR CODY	WHAT IS ____?
THIS NEW MEXICO TOWN WAS NAMED FOR THE GRAVE MARKERS OF SOME OF ITS EARLIER SETTLERS	WHAT IS ____?
SKINNER'S MUDHOLE IS A NICKNAME OF THIS OREGON CITY; IT WAS NAMED FOR MR. SKINNER	WHAT IS ____?
STOCK UP ON BREATH MINTS BEFORE HEADING TO GILROY, CALIF., WORLD CAPITAL OF THIS PUNGENT BULB	WHAT IS ____?
BUTTE, MONTANA, LIES ON THIS "DIVIDE" THAT SEPARATES NORTH AMERICA'S EAST- & WEST-RUNNING RIVERS	WHAT IS ____?

AUSTIN
BRANSON
CALIFORNIA
CAPE LOOKOUT
CHEYENNE
DEVILS TOWER
FLAGSTAFF
GILA RIVER
GRAND TETON
GREEN RIVER
HANNIBAL
LAKE OZARK
LAKE TAHOE
NAVAJO NATION
OLYMPIA

PRESCOTT
PUGET SOUND
SIOUX CITY
ST. LOUIS
TULSA
WHITEFISH LAKE

D	E	V	I	L	S	T	O	W	E	R	L	E	F	O	T	A
R	T	L	A	U	S	T	I	N	Q	K	O	L	L	B	D	D
V	T	A	W	F	X	A	E	Z	J	H	A	Y	R	J	S	Q
M	O	S	J	X	R	K	M	E	A	G	M	A	I	I	S	N
N	C	C	I	L	R	A	G	T	S	P	N	C	U	J	O	H
O	S	R	C	C	J	N	E	T	I	S	Q	O	C	T	X	P
I	E	U	A	E	K	K	A	A	O	P	L	N	E	R	C	U
T	R	C	P	T	A	F	J	N	E	T	I	T	L	E	H	G
A	P	E	E	L	F	I	P	S	S	U	D	I	A	V	E	E
N	A	S	L	U	T	Y	N	I	S	N	G	N	B	I	Y	T
O	W	Y	O	M	I	N	G	R	A	D	X	E	I	R	E	S
J	N	T	O	L	X	X	R	R	O	A	V	N	N	N	N	O
A	I	Y	K	Y	X	K	G	H	A	F	H	T	N	E	N	U
V	S	I	O	U	X	C	I	T	Y	H	I	A	A	E	E	N
A	I	M	U	K	R	A	Z	O	E	K	A	L	H	R	J	D
N	S	Y	T	G	I	L	A	R	I	V	E	R	A	G	F	L
W	H	I	T	E	F	I	S	H	L	A	K	E	O	C	V	X

Answers on page 145.

SHAKESPEARE

THIS SHAKESPEARE CHARACTER SPEAKS OF THE "POMP AND CIRCUMSTANCE" OF WAR TO IAGO	WHO IS ____?
IN "HENRY IV, PART II", A HOSTESS COMPLAINS THAT THIS KNIGHT HAS "EATEN ME OUT OF HOUSE AND HOME"	WHO IS ____?
TRINCULO & CALIBAN MAKE "STRANGE BEDFELLOWS" IN THIS ROMANCE	WHAT IS ____?
WHEN HE MISTAKES FRANKNESS FOR LACK OF AFFECTION, THIS KING REJECTS HIS ONLY LOYAL DAUGHTER	WHO IS ____?
THE KING'S CASTLE IN THIS DANISH SEAPORT IS THE SETTING FOR MOST OF "HAMLET"	WHAT IS ____?

ACROSS

1 LIGHT BULB GAS
6 CITY BUILT ON SEVEN HILLS
10 NEW DEAL PRES.
13 ANKLEBONES
14 DIRECTOR KAZAN
15 ALL THERE UPSTAIRS
16
18 CITY PLANNER'S MAP
19 ANGRY FEELING
20 AVERAGE GRADE
21 IS SO INCLINED
23 CAMPER'S LIGHT
25 "___ LATE THAN NEVER"
26 SEMI-SERIOUS "I SEE"
27 WHAT "STIFLE" IS AN ANAGRAM OF
30 BERMUDA SETTING: ABBR.
31 GYM PAD
33 PINOCCHIO'S GOLDFISH
34 MIL. POSTS
35 BARELY GOT (WITH "OUT")
37 "...AGAINST A ___ OF

TROUBLES": HAMLET
38 FOOTBALL OFFICIALS, BRIEFLY
40 "ALADDIN" HERO
41 ADAM SMITH'S SUBJ.
43 MD'S ORG.
44 EMPLOYEE ID, OFTEN
45 "STATELY PLEASURE-DOME" OF VERSE
47 OFFSHOOT DENOMINATION
51 SEAL ENGRAVED ON A RING
53
55 LOOSENS, AS SNEAKERS
57 "SIMPSONS" BARTENDER
58 CALL BEFORE A "DO-OVER" SERVE
59 BUBBLY BRAND
60 VISIBLY EMBARRASSED
63 HISTORIC PERIODS
64 SMALL CASE FOR PINS AND NEEDLES
65 NOT AT ALL WORDY
66 SUN. MORNING TALK
67 NOTHING, IN NANTES
68 MORE CRAFTY

DOWN

1 HISTORIC HUN
2 FULL OF THAT OLD SCHOOL SPIRIT
3 SALAD VEGGIES
4 BONE: PREFIX
5 ELEANOR ROOSEVELT, TO TEDDY
6 ADMONITION TO SINNERS
7 "BRAVO!" AT A BULLFIGHT
8 CATCHALL CATEGORY, BRIEFLY
9 FIT TO CONSUME
10
11 THEY'RE USED TO DETERMINE PATERNITY
12 SNAPPY COMEBACKS
15 YOUNG BARRACUDA
17 KIND OF BADGE FOR A SCOUT
22 MEND ONE'S WAYS
24 BIG BOOK
28 LA SCALA SEGMENT
29 HIGHEST NOTE, OLD STYLE
32 MADISON AVE. VIP
35
36
37 BEN, TO JERRY STILLER
39 FREEDOM FROM WORRIES
40 PRESUPPOSES
42 PARTY FOOD PROVIDER
43 STEPHEN KING'S CHRISTINE, AND OTHERS
46 GODADDY PURCHASE
48 QUEEN OF MYSTERIES
49 "MONTY PYTHON" COMIC JOHN
50 BE SHAKY ON ONE'S FEET
52 COLE AND TURNER
54 MICROWAVES, AS LEFTOVERS
56 ORG. LOOKING FOR ALIENS
61 EXPECTED SOON
62 ACTRESS BARBARA ___ GEDDES

Answers on page 146.

WITTY QUOTES

THIS BALTIMORE SAGE WROTE, "INJUSTICE IS RELATIVELY EASY TO BEAR; WHAT STINGS IS JUSTICE"

WHO WAS ____?

HE SAID TO JAMES BOSWELL, "YOU HAVE BUT TWO TOPICS, YOURSELF AND ME. I AM SICK OF BOTH"

WHO WAS ____?

ALEXANDER WOOLLCOTT CALLED THIS ROUND TABLE WIT A COMBINATION "OF LITTLE NELL AND LADY MACBETH"

WHO WAS ____?

THIS AUTHOR NOTED, "RADICAL CHIC… IS ONLY RADICAL IN STYLE; IN ITS HEART IT IS PART OF SOCIETY"

WHO IS ____?

WHEN THIS NEW YORK YANKEE WAS ASKED, "WHAT TIME IS IT?" HE ANSWERED, "YOU MEAN NOW?"

WHO IS ____?

(find all words set in capitals)

"I NEVER DARE to WRITE as FUNNY as I CAN"

—Oliver Wendell Holmes, Sr.

"JESTERS do OFTEN PROVE PROPHETS"

—William Shakespeare

"**JOKING DECIDES GREAT THINGS, STRONGER and BETTER oft THAN EARNEST can.**"

—**John Milton**

"**LAUGH and be FAT**"

—**John Taylor**

"**ONLY MAN can be ABSURD: for only man can be DIGNIFIED.**"

—**G.K. Chesterton**

S	T	R	O	N	G	E	R	A	E	Z	O	K	I	G	O	K
A	E	F	M	D	G	E	G	G	B	P	R	O	V	E	S	T
M	R	D	T	N	V	H	H	S	F	S	E	T	I	R	W	S
U	A	A	I	E	H	R	E	M	G	O	U	X	H	K	E	E
E	D	K	N	C	S	B	F	T	R	F	F	R	W	A	I	N
L	O	H	U	D	E	P	L	H	E	Z	N	T	D	T	N	R
J	R	L	G	T	M	D	O	I	A	F	Y	U	E	K	J	A
O	Z	X	T	U	W	W	W	N	T	P	B	G	J	N	C	E
H	P	E	K	I	A	B	M	G	O	F	N	N	O	N	L	Y
N	R	J	A	U	H	L	O	S	J	E	S	T	E	R	S	O
S	O	A	D	O	R	O	T	H	Y	P	A	R	K	E	R	G
O	P	V	A	U	M	J	Z	N	Y	Y	C	H	N	I	R	I
N	H	L	M	E	N	C	K	E	N	Z	N	I	O	A	E	B
E	E	D	E	I	F	I	N	G	I	D	O	N	H	Y	C	E
S	T	Y	B	M	L	D	C	W	I	M	F	F	U	B	C	R
J	S	U	G	J	V	I	H	U	A	T	A	U	T	F	D	R
G	M	N	W	P	A	D	C	N	H	D	T	E	Q	R	M	A

Answers on page 146.

WEIRD NATURE

THESE UNGULATES HAVE A THIRD EYELID TO PROTECT THEIR EYES FROM BLOWING SAND	WHAT ARE ____?
ALHA 81005, THE 1st METEORITE PROVEN TO HAVE COME FROM THE MOON, WAS FOUND ON THIS CONTINENT	WHAT IS ____?
AIRBORNE GRAINS FROM TREES, GRASS OR WEEDS, IT MAY PRODUCE HAY FEVER ATTACKS	WHAT IS ____?
THE "HORNS" OF THE GREAT HORNED OWL ARE ACTUALLY MADE OF THESE	WHAT ARE ____?
CRICKETS "HEAR" VIA HIGHLY SENSITIVE MEMBRANES ON THESE BODY PARTS	WHAT ARE ____?

ACROSS

1 FIRST ISRAELI AMBASSADOR TO THE UN ABBA ___
5 GULLY FILLERS
10 PUT ___ ON (LIMIT)
14 UNCOMMON, AVIS-WISE
15 BERT'S MUPPET BUDDY
16 FRENCH SAILOR AND WRITER PIERRE
17
19 "SPAMALOT" CREATOR IDLE
20 CRACK, AS A SECRET MESSAGE
21 ALIENS, FOR SHORT
23 BUMP-LOG LINK
24 HOMES FOR GENIES
25 ARTIST'S PORTFOLIO
27 SINGER DIFRANCO
28 AMAZON'S SMART HOME DEVICE
31
32 "LARGEMOUTH" FISH
34 UNIV.'S COUSIN

36 SAN ___ (SILICON VALLEY CITY)
37 SPEAK IN FLOWERY LANGUAGE
40 GAMAL ___ NASSER OF EGYPT
43 THEREFORE, IN A PROOF
44 LIKE LOOK-ALIKES
48 EMULATES RIP VAN WINKLE
50 ABBR. ON A CORNERSTONE
52 GOLD INGOT
53
55 CAUSING GOOSE BUMPS, MAYBE
57 COMMUNICATION SYST. FOR THE DEAF
58 "ISLAND HOME" SINGER CHRISTINE
59
61 Q QUEUE?
63 ALI BABA'S MAGICAL COMMAND
66 FRIENDS, IN FRANCE
67 FORMER ATTORNEY GENERAL JANET AND A NEVADA CITY
68 "TIME ___ A PREMIUM"
69 CAPITOL VIPS
70 BOSS'S NERVOUSNESS-INDUCING NOTE
71 EUROPE'S LARGEST VOLCANO

DOWN

1 SWING OR VICTORIAN, E.G.
2 COWBOY'S NECKWEAR
3 GREEK GODDESS OF THE MOON
4 RACIAL EQUALITY GP.
5 STAMP FOR AN INCOMING PKG.
6 PRADO WORKS
7 ENDING OF SOME PASTA NAMES
8 MORE AFFABLE
9 HUB FOR ALASKA AIRLINES
10 POPULAR DRAFT PICK
11 HEADGEAR FOR A PRINCE
12 LIKE A FORMERLY ASLEEP FOOT
13 "GUERNICA" PAINTER
18 FLOWER FOR VALENTINE'S DAY
22 HINDU SAGE
24 CHEMIST'S HANGOUT
25 "___ CLAIBORNE" (1992 STEPHEN KING NOVEL)
26 COLORFUL APPLE COMPUTERS
29 210, TO CLAUDIUS
30 IT "SPRINGS ETERNAL"
33 LIKE CANDY
35
38 DOMINANT, IN A WOLF PACK
39 ONE OF THE SANDBOX SET
40 TO THE EXTENT THAT
41 CONFESSIONAL OPENING
42 GAVE A HAND TO
45 SIDE BY SIDE
46 GUY WHO'S ALWAYS GOT YOUR BACK
47 OLD "BEFORE"
49 MADRID MISTERS
51 "TAKE THIS OUT," IN PROOFREADING
54 MADRAS MONEY
56 BORDEN MASCOT
59 ___ PENH, CAMBODIAN CITY
60 BONE: PREFIX
62 LETTERS AT THE START OF A DESTROYER'S NAME
64 HOUSTON-TO-BOSTON DIR.
65 AIRPORT INFO, INFORMALLY

Answers on page 146.

WOMEN AUTHORS

Clue	Response
SHE TURNED HER SHORT STORY COLLECTION "WIND AND WATER" INTO THE BESTSELLER "THE JOY LUCK CLUB"	WHO IS ____?
LAST NAME OF PATRICIA HIGHSMITH'S "TALENTED" TITLE TOM WHO GETS AWAY WITH MURDER	WHAT IS ____?
AROUND HALLOWEEN ONE OF HER FAN CLUBS HOSTS A "GATHERING OF THE ANCIENTS" PARTY IN NEW ORLEANS	WHO IS ____?
VIRGINIA WOOLF ORIGINALLY CALLED HER "MRS. DALLOWAY" NOVEL THIS, AS DID THE 2002 NICOLE KIDMAN FILM	WHAT IS ____?
"WHITE TEETH", A 2000 BESTSELLER BY THIS WOMAN, IS A NOVEL ABOUT 2 LONDON FAMILIES	WHO IS ____?

AGATHA CHRISTIE	GEORGE ELIOT	JODI PICOULT
ALICE WALKER	GILLIAN FLYNN	JOY HARJO
ANGELA CARTER	J.K. ROWLING	MAYA ANGELOU
DORIS LESSING	JANE AUSTEN	MEG CABOT
GAIL GODWIN	JOAN DIDION	SUE MILLER

SUSAN CHOI
SUSAN SONTAG
~~TONI MORRISON~~

P	F	H	S	R	X	P	A	G	O	S	C	R	O	G	V	O
E	C	I	R	E	N	N	A	A	G	U	P	K	R	D	J	X
P	J	G	U	L	Z	A	D	I	E	S	M	I	T	H	A	G
N	O	N	O	L	L	T	M	L	O	A	E	Y	M	A	T	N
O	A	I	H	I	P	O	P	G	R	N	S	R	J	L	L	I
S	N	L	E	M	A	B	Y	O	G	S	P	E	S	I	U	S
I	D	W	H	E	M	A	B	D	E	O	L	T	U	C	O	S
R	I	O	T	U	Y	C	T	W	E	N	G	R	S	E	C	E
R	D	R	Y	S	T	G	I	I	L	T	L	A	A	W	I	L
O	I	K	Y	C	A	E	Z	N	I	A	M	C	N	A	P	S
M	O	J	J	Y	N	M	E	G	O	G	Z	A	C	L	I	I
I	N	J	A	N	E	A	U	S	T	E	N	L	H	K	D	R
N	N	Y	L	F	N	A	I	L	L	I	G	E	O	E	O	O
O	M	A	Y	A	A	N	G	E	L	O	U	G	I	R	J	D
T	Z	A	K	M	O	I	A	P	E	J	N	N	G	I	X	C
V	B	Y	E	L	P	I	R	J	O	Y	H	A	R	J	O	O
E	I	T	S	I	R	H	C	A	H	T	A	G	A	E	Y	U

Answers on page 147.

WORLD CAPITALS

THE NOBEL PEACE PRIZE IS THE ONLY ONE OF THE NOBEL PRIZES THAT'S AWARDED IN THIS CAPITAL	WHAT IS ____?
THIS CAPITAL IN THE VALLEY OF NEPAL IS AT AN ALTITUDE OF ABOUT 4,000 FEET	WHAT IS ____?
THIS CITY IN MOROCCO CONTAINS THE NEVER-COMPLETED HASSAN TOWER	WHAT IS ____?
IT WAS THE BIRTHPLACE OF SAMUEL GOLDWYN & MARIE CURIE	WHAT IS ____?
MUHAMMAD ALI'S "RUMBLE IN THE JUNGLE" WAS FOUGHT IN THIS CITY, AT THE TIME THE CAPITAL OF ZAIRE	WHAT IS ____?

ALGIERS
ATHENS
BEIJING
BRASILIA
BRUSSELS
BUDAPEST
DAMASCUS
HANOI
HAVANA
KABUL
LIMA
LISBON
LOME
LUANDA
MINSK

OTTAWA
QUITO
ROSEAU
SANTIAGO
SOFIA
TEHRAN

K	B	Q	Q	U	P	O	S	N	U	U	N	F	A	R	F	W
S	U	Z	A	W	B	L	Z	K	M	X	Z	X	N	X	Z	A
N	F	K	P	A	T	H	E	N	S	L	A	Z	A	N	K	S
I	E	T	M	X	E	S	A	W	A	T	T	O	V	H	O	R
M	Q	I	S	D	A	W	A	A	I	L	I	S	A	R	B	A
N	L	S	F	A	S	A	H	S	N	I	K	N	H	R	U	W
H	J	S	L	K	N	K	P	V	Y	W	O	Q	A	D	N	Z
U	A	Z	R	E	A	T	N	U	P	I	Q	B	N	Q	S	C
A	H	D	N	E	S	B	I	T	R	U	A	A	U	Q	U	W
I	R	G	N	L	I	S	U	A	E	T	M	I	D	S	C	P
F	U	Q	N	A	L	G	U	L	G	H	T	L	O	D	S	V
O	A	U	H	I	U	O	L	R	T	O	R	S	F	R	A	E
S	E	Y	S	X	J	L	G	A	B	D	L	A	A	W	M	P
D	S	B	Q	K	C	I	K	Z	W	O	A	V	N	O	A	V
V	O	I	Z	V	T	S	E	P	A	D	U	B	L	L	D	C
N	R	D	S	W	C	D	R	B	O	N	K	U	C	X	Y	F
X	V	L	A	K	A	G	R	H	U	Q	W	I	G	D	U	O

Answers on page 147.

WORLD HISTORY

HIS FORCES TOOK THE CAPITAL OF THE SUNG DYNASTY IN 1276 & WITHIN 3 YEARS HE CONTROLLED ALL OF CHINA	WHO IS ____?
AMONG THOSE TO REACH THIS AFRICAN OUTPOST IN THE 19TH CENTURY WERE RENE CAILLIE & GORDON LAING	WHAT IS ____?
IN 1192 JAPAN'S EMPEROR GAVE MILITARY LEADER YORITOMO THIS TITLE WHICH MEANS "GREAT GENERAL"	WHAT IS ____?
15th CENTURY EMPEROR MEHMED II IS KNOWN TO HISTORY BY THIS EPITHET, LIKE KING WILLIAM I OF ENGLAND	WHAT IS ____?
FROM THE GREEK FOR "PHOENICIAN", THIS WORD DESCRIBES THE 3 ROME VS. CARTHAGE WARS	WHAT IS ____?

ACROSS

1 "NO ___, NO FOUL"
5 ENLIVEN
10 LASSES' COUNTERPARTS
14 FRENZIED WAY TO RUN
15 BASEBALL HALL OF FAMER EDD
16 REGION
17 WINNER OF 26 OSCARS
19 NEWSPAPER OPINION PIECE
20
21 POSSIBLE ANSWER TO "IS THAT YOU?"
23 OVERHEAD TRAINS
24 IV DOSAGE AMTS.
26 ONLINE CHATS, FOR SHORT
27
33 SKEWERED THAI DISH
36 FATHER OF OEDIPUS
37 ENDING FOR "RANCH"
38 GENTLY-WORN, AS CLOTHES

39 FAR FROM TALKATIVE
40 BOAT BACKS
41 COMB INSECT
42 "NO ___, BOB!"
43 CHEESE OR CHARD
44 SHORTEST PRESIDENT
47 DEGREE IN RELIGION
48 TRANSMISSION TYPE: ABBR.
49 VENOMOUS SERPENT
52 STEVENSON'S ISLAND
57 ___ PORK: CHINESE DISH WITH PANCAKES
59 SLEDDING SLOPE
60
62 "WOULD YOU CARE FOR ANYTHING ___?"
63 RIVER NEAR THE VATICAN
64 TRICKSTER OF NORSE MYTH
65 DASHING STYLE
66 RETRACT A COMMENT
67 "NEVER WAVE AT ___" (ROSALIND RUSSELL FLICK)

DOWN

1 ANCHOR ROPE HOLE
2 "___ AND THE NIGHT VISITORS" (MENOTTI OPERA)
3 HERSHEY CARAMEL CANDIES
4 DEPT. THAT WORKS WITH SALES
5 "PURPLE RAIN" SINGER
6 DAWN GODDESS
7 SMALL AND WEAK
8 LAWSUIT BENEFACTOR
9 MR. AMERICA'S SOURCE OF PRIDE
10 FOUNDER OF TAOISM
11 SOME DADA PAINTINGS
12 CONSIDER TO BE
13 "NO ORDINARY LOVE" SINGER
18 SMALL STATE RULED BY A SOVEREIGN
22 DON OF RADIO FAME
25 EYEBALL COVERING
27 INSIGNIFICANT AMOUNT
28 ROWED, AS A BOAT
29 SOME JAPANESE-AMERICANS
30 GET A NEW MORTGAGE, BRIEFLY
31 FOOD CRUMBS
32 COLONIAL FLAGMAKER
33 PREDICATE'S PARTNER: ABBR.
34 NOT ASHORE
35 BE CRAWLING (WITH)
39
40 BEARD ON BARLEY
42 AIR FRANCE RETIREES OF '03
43 "ME TOO"
45 BIG SUR INSTITUTE
46 NAMESAKE OF MANY CHURCHES
49 PUT ON ___ (ENTERTAIN)
50 ZULU WARRIOR KING
51
52 QUAKER'S "YOU"
53 LITTLE STREAM
54 MAXWELL OR SCHIAPARELLI
55 DAMAGE IRREPARABLY
56 DIES DOWN
58 THE SOONER ST.
61 MEADOW, IN VERSE

Answers on page 147.

ANAGRAMMED WORLD LEADERS

RUSSIAN AROUND: RIVAL DUMP IN IT	WHO IS ____?
THINK OF ENGLAND: HEARTY MESA	WHO IS ____?
BOSS IN BERLIN: MAKE ALLERGEN	WHO IS ____?
OH, CANADA: ADJURE NUT SUIT	WHO IS ____?
HAVANA BAD TIME: RURAL COAST	WHO IS ____?

BENJAMIN NETANYAHU
DONALD TRUMP
EMMANUEL MACRON
ENRIQUE PEÑA NIETO
HAIDER AL-ABADI
HASSAN ROUHANI
JACOB ZUMA
KIM JONG-UN
MALCOLM TURNBULL
MOON JAE-IN
NARENDRA MODI
RODRIGO DUTERTE
SHINZO ABE
XI JINPING

X	G	S	S	F	D	O	N	A	L	D	T	R	U	M	P	N
O	T	E	I	N	A	N	E	P	E	U	Q	I	R	N	E	W
B	E	N	J	A	M	I	N	N	E	T	A	N	Y	A	H	U
R	O	D	R	I	G	O	D	U	T	E	R	T	E	A	G	G
I	I	N	A	H	U	O	R	N	A	S	S	A	H	V	F	K
N	A	R	E	N	D	R	A	M	O	D	I	H	H	R	P	P
M	N	O	R	C	A	M	L	E	U	N	A	M	M	E	N	E
M	A	L	C	O	L	M	T	U	R	N	B	U	L	L	B	K
A	N	G	E	L	A	M	E	R	K	E	L	Q	N	A	O	I
U	A	E	D	U	R	T	N	I	T	S	U	J	O	V	N	M
R	K	T	H	E	R	E	S	A	M	A	Y	Z	L	K	S	J
E	U	N	I	E	A	J	N	O	O	M	N	F	E	O	Y	O
U	R	M	U	V	L	A	D	I	M	I	R	P	U	T	I	N
A	M	U	Z	B	O	C	A	J	H	D	K	Q	T	V	T	G
L	H	R	A	U	L	C	A	S	T	R	O	R	D	J	S	U
L	J	K	D	S	R	X	I	J	I	N	P	I	N	G	A	N
L	W	S	O	H	A	I	D	E	R	A	L	A	B	A	D	I

Answers on page 148.

FEMALE INVENTORS

MAYBE IT WAS BAD WEATHER IN 1903 WHEN MARY ANDERSON CREATED THIS DEVICE FOR CARS	WHAT IS ____?
AFTER A CHEMICAL SPILL AT 3M, PATSY SHERMAN HELPED CREATE THIS VERSATILE FABRIC STAIN REPELLANT	WHAT IS ____?
POLICEMEN CAN THANK STEPHANIE KWOLEK FOR HER INVENTION OF THIS TOUGHER-THAN-STEEL POLYMER FIBER	WHAT IS ____?
IN 1859 MARTHA COSTON PATENTED THESE DEVICES THAT SAILORS COULD SEND INTO THE SKY TO COMMUNICATE	WHAT ARE ____?
ANN MOORE INVENTED THIS BABY CARRIER AFTER SEEING WOMEN IN TOGO CARRY THEIR BABIES IN FABRIC SLINGS	WHAT IS ____?

APGAR SCORE
CIRCULAR SAW
COFFEE FILTER
COLOR ORGAN
CORSET
CURVED CORALS
DOUBLE-CROSTIC
FRUIT PRESS
GREEN STEEL
HABERMAN FEEDER
HEARST PATTERNS
HUG BOX
HYDYNE
JONES PROCESS
K BRICK

LIQUID PAPER
MICRO-ELECTRODE
PH ELECTRODE
PUNCTOGRAPH
REEL
RESPIRATOR
SOLAR ENERGY
THREE-D IMAGING

N E Q W H E A R S T P A T T E R N S M
Z R T A H U G B O X D V J V R E J X B
C O H S G V U S E R A L F L A N G I S
K C R R E P A P D I U Q I L L A Y K C
H S E A R O T A R I P S E R V G Z C Z
D R E L D Y E I V E P E G S E R F I J
P A D U E L V R U F R F E M K O R R R
C G I C L P V L E E T S N E E R G B D
U P M R A S O D X I A T E S R O C K R
R A A I S S E R P T I U R F N L F W A
V B G C C I T S O R C E L B U O D M G
E N I B E D O R T C E I E O R C I M H
D S N R Z J V S O L A R E N E R G Y C
C N G P H E L E C T R O D E Y V D X T
O U C O F F E E F I L T E R O D J Y O
R G P U N C T O G R A P H Z Q X Y J C
A L H A B E R M A N F E E D E R D H S
L I W I N D S H I E L D W I P E R G S
S J O N E S P R O C E S S U L A O S Q

Answers on page 148.

10-LETTER WORDS

COLORFUL TERM FOR A PERSON WHO FORGES OBJECTS OF IRON	WHAT IS ____?
REPUGNANTLY HATEFUL; NOTHING PERSONAL AGAINST THE "SNOWMAN"	WHAT IS ____?
TO GO ABOUT UNDER FALSE PRETENSES, OR A TYPE OF PARTY WITH HISTORICAL COSTUMES	WHAT IS ____?
THE INTERNET OR THE ONLINE WORLD	WHAT IS ____?
A SAPSUCKER IS ONE OF THESE BIRDS	WHAT IS ____?

ACROSS

1 PART OF A WINDOW
5 RUSSIAN MOUNTAINS
9 HEALTH ORGS.
13
16 QUITE A LOT
17 LIKE AN ESPECIALLY TASTY DISH
18 CONCORDE FLEET, ONCE
19 "___ SAY IT?"
20 U.S. 1 AND U.S. 66
22 AFRICAN TEA LEAVES POPULAR IN SCRABBLE
23 POINTER SISTERS "___ EXCITED"
25 STUDY, WITH "ON"
27 KING ARTHUR'S WAS ROUND
30 "___ GIVEN SUNDAY" (PACINO FOOTBALL FILM)
32 HAVE REGRETS OVER
33 MAGIC, ON A SCOREBOARD

34 BODY THAT INCLUDES SHAPE
36 CANNON LOADER
39 ITALIAN "ONES"
41
43 FOOTBALL LEGEND KNUTE
45 MORMON CHURCH INITS.
46 WHERE TO SEE MT. RUSHMORE
47 HYUNDAI RIVAL
48 LETTERS ON SOME PARTY INVITATIONS
49 ___ KEYBOARD (TYPES)
50 HOPE TO ACHIEVE
52 COMPUTER GAME SET ON AN ISLAND
54 THUMB, AS A RIDE
55 EASY WIN
57 REALLY FUNNY
60 TENNIS SITUATION AFTER DEUCE
62
65 BUILDING LOT
66 SETTING APART
67 AREA IN LONDON OR NEW YORK CITY
68 CLEAN AND TIDY
69 DROPPED IN THE MAIL

DOWN

1 APARTMENT, SLANGILY
2 LIKE MANY OF US AT MIDNIGHT
3 THE BIG EASY, FAMILIARLY
4 FOOD NETWORK'S "___ LIVE"
5 THEY'RE AGAINST
6 WHEN DOUBLED, ONE OF THE TELETUBBIES
7 INC. OR LTD.
8 VOLUNTEER'S OFFER
9 ___ "PINAFORE" (COMIC OPERA)
10
11 LIKE DRAFT BEER
12 KIND OF ANALYST: ABBR.
14 HOCKEY PLAYERS
15 WIDE SHOE SIZE
21 ACTRESS GILBERT AND POET TEASDALE
24 LIKE CHEERIOS, SAY
26 SELLS IN A BEAR MARKET
27 TRAVEL BY BUS, SAY
28 CARTOONIST PETER
29
31 IN A HIGH-MINDED WAY
35 POWER SERVE, PERHAPS
36 AMTRAK AND B&O
37 HIGH ANDES PLANTS
38 METRIC PREFIX MEANING TEN
40 PLAY SPORADICALLY, LIKE A CD
42 LAND CONQUERED BY DAVID
44 "WE WEAR SHORT SHORTS" BRAND
10 SING THE BLUES ABOUT
49 WEDDING SEATER
50 TV SOUND SIGNAL
51 T. ___ PRICE (INVESTMENT FIRM)
53 BOTHER WITH BARKS, PUPPY-STYLE
54 FOUR-STRING GUITAR
56 LOOK CAREFULLY (OVER)
58 DUST-BOWL MIGRANT
59 AL GORE'S STATE, BRIEFLY
61 KEANU'S ROLE IN "THE MATRIX"
63 ABBR. AFTER ELIZABETH WARREN'S NAME
64 COL.'S OUTFIT

Answers on page 148.

FICTIONAL CHARACTERS

Clue	Answer
SPOILER ALERT: THIS MARCH SISTER DIES IN "LITTLE WOMEN"	WHO IS ____?
THIS E.B. WHITE CHARACTER SLEPT IN A TINY BED MADE OF "FOUR CLOTHESPINS AND A CIGARETTE BOX"	WHO IS ____?
IN "THE WIZARD OF OZ", DOROTHY LIVED WITH AUNT EM & THIS UNCLE, A FARMER	WHO IS ____?
ON OCT. 2, 1872, HE & HIS SERVANT LEAVE LONDON IN AN ATTEMPT TO GO AROUND THE WORLD IN 80 DAYS	WHO IS ____?
SELF-DESCRIBED "SINGLETON" WHOSE BESTSELLING "DIARY" WAS CONCOCTED BY HELEN FIELDING	WHO IS ____?

ASH WILLIAMS
AUGIE MARCH
BENNY PROFANE
BEOWULF
COLONEL KURTZ
CTHULHU
GUY MONTAG
HOLDEN CAULFIELD
IGNATIUS REILLY
KEYSER SOZE
KILGORE TROUT
MARTY MCFLY
OEDIPA MAAS
OSCAR WAO
PAP FINN

PIRATE PRENTICE
RABBIT ANGSTROM
SETHE
SWITTERS
TORU OKADA

```
R R A B B I T A N G S T R O M K T
E Y B E N N Y P R O F A N E Z E E
S R C O L O N E L K U R T Z E Y X
E N A S H W I L L I A M S Y H S H
N E H T E S O S C A R W A O K E T
O H D A U G I E M A R C H I G R E
J E O E D I P A M A A S L G E S B
T L C T H U L H U A A G L R B O K
E C S R E T T I W S O Y L A Y Z G
G N P I R A T E P R E N T I C E A
D U F F P H I L E A S F O G G X T
I H Y V E L T T I L T N A U T S N
R Y L L I E R S U I T A N G I F O
B W S N R O U P G N N I F P A P M
B E O W U L F M A R T Y M C F L Y
X U J T O R U O K A D A G E N E U
H O L D E N C A U L F I E L D B G
```


Answers on page 149.

ANIMAL WORDS

AN ADULT MALE DEER, OR A TYPE OF PARTY BEFORE A WEDDING	WHAT IS ____?
IF YOU'RE PLAGUED BY ONE OF THESE ON YOUR BACK, YOU'VE GOT PROBLEMS, MAN, BIG PROBLEMS	WHAT IS ____?
STEPPING UP TO THE PLATE? TRY ONE OF THESE MAMMALS OF THE ORDER CHIROPTERA	WHAT IS ____?
TO COMPLAIN PEEVISHLY, OR A FISH	WHAT IS ____?
A QUARRELSOME WOMAN; ONE MIGHT EVEN SAY SHE'S VULPINE	WHAT IS ____?

ACROSS

1
5 SNEEZIN' REASONS
10 WHEAT OR SOYBEANS
14 HOME OF THE ROCK AND ROLL HALL OF FAME
15 SKIN-SOOTHING INGREDIENTS
16 DANCE PERFORMED IN GRASS SKIRTS
17 FAT IN THE CAN?
18 HOLY BOOK
19 BIRD OF THE NILE
20 FADE-OUT, IN MOVIES
22 SHOE LIKE A CLOG
23 FENCER'S BLADE
24 HUMOROUS WORD FOR "THINK"
26 REPORTERS' ANGLES
29 JEEVES'S BOSS, FORMALLY
32 ACCENT OVER AN "N"

1	2	3	4	■	5	6	7	8	9	■	10	11	12	13
14				■	15					■	16			
17				■	18					■	19			
20				21			■	■	22					
■	■	■	23			■	24	25					■	■
26	27	28			■	■	29						30	31
32					■	33	34			■	35			
36			■	37	38					39	■	40		
41			42	■	43				■	44	45			
46				47			■	■	48					
■	■	49					■	50				■	■	■
51	52				■	■	53					54	55	56
57				■	58	59				■	60			
61				■	62					■	63			
64				■	65					■	66			

33 BUT, IN BERLIN
35 BIT OF DATA
36 EMINEM'S GENRE
37 LINEN FABRICS
40 DIVISION OF ABOUT ONE BILLION YEARS
41 "SNAKE EYES" PAIR
43 ANGLER'S HOPE
44 ILL-GOTTEN PROFIT
46 VICTORIA'S SECRET PURCHASE
48
49 TESTS SOMETHING'S WEIGHT BY LIFTING
50 GIRL IN A KILT
51 DOESN'T GO ON
53 REAGAN'S DECADE
57
58
60 WANDER FAR AND WIDE
61 AUTHOR SARAH ___ JEWETT
62 SPIN DOCTOR'S CONCERN
63 FILLS WITH WONDER
64 DICK TRACY'S LOVE
65 SKY STREAKER
66 QUARTERBACK'S SPECIALTY

DOWN

1 "GONE!" AT AUCTIONS
2 PEANUT-SAUCE CUISINE
3 MAKES KNOWN, AS GRIEVANCES
4 UNEXPECTED BLESSING
5 SENDS A TELEGRAPH TO
6 POPEYE'S OYL
7 EAR OR BRAIN SECTION
8 ITS CAP IS DOVER
9 CHICAGO-TO-MIAMI DIR.
10 ITALIAN TABLE WINE
11 GAWK ON THE HIGHWAY
12 LITTLE BIT OF EVERYTHING MIX
13 TIME TRAVELER'S DESTINATION
21 MADE A CHOICE
22 PAUL MCCARTNEY'S TITLE
24 BEYOND ROTUND
25 MAKE COFFEE, IN A WAY
26 BARBER'S SHARPENER
27 TROPICAL VINE
28 SWISS HERDERS' INSTRUMENTS
30 "...AND I'LL BE IN SCOTLAND ___ YE"
31 POUNDS AND MARKS
33 NOT QUITE RIGHT
34
38 HELP WITH THE HEIST
39 WALK THROUGH MELTING SNOW
42 PLAINS OF SIBERIA
45 REMOVE, AS FROM A CAR SEAT
47 NO ___, ANDS OR BUTS
48 FRIDGE DECORATION
50 FEUDAL LORD, OR HIS SUBJECT
51 CONNERY, BY BIRTH
52 SHIPPING WEIGHT ALLOWANCE
53 FINAL OR MIDTERM
54 "FIELD OF DREAMS" SETTING
55 NIGHTS BEFORE HOLIDAYS
56 PSYCHIATRIST'S APPT.
58 LONDON THEATRE, THE OLD ___
59 "AS I SEE IT," IN AN EMAIL

Answers on page 149.

FROM THE LATIN FOR...

..."TO PULL", ON THE FARM IT COMES IN WHEEL & CRAWLER TYPES	WHAT IS ____?
..."SUBSTITUTE", THE TYPE OF MOTHERHOOD IN THE COURT CASE "IN THE MATTER OF BABY M"	WHAT IS ____?
..."NATIVE COUNTRY", IT'S RETURNING A REFUGEE OR P.O.W. TO HIS OR HER HOMELAND	WHAT IS ____?
..."AROUND", IN RECORDING IT'S THE NATURAL ACOUSTICS OF THE ROOM	WHAT IS ____?
..."POUR" OR "MELT", IT'S AN ESTABLISHMENT WHERE METAL IS CAST IN MOLDS	WHAT IS ____?

ACUMEN
AGENDA
ALTRUISM
ATROCITY
AVARICE
CHIVALROUS
CREPUSCULAR
CULL
FACSIMILE
FLUX
FUTILE
INSIPID
LANGUID
MODICUM
MORIBUND

NAÏVE
PARVENU
PERTURB
PUERILE
REPRISAL
SACROSANCT
SIMULACRUM
SUCCUMB
TURPITUDE
UBIQUITY

K	Q	Y	R	D	N	U	O	F	R	W	P	E	H	E	A	F
S	U	O	R	L	A	V	I	H	C	O	X	L	L	E	L	X
Q	N	R	E	P	R	I	S	A	L	C	O	I	N	D	T	J
I	E	O	M	O	R	I	B	U	N	D	T	R	E	U	R	S
M	V	T	K	X	V	A	J	X	B	U	N	E	M	T	U	A
O	R	C	C	M	Y	N	L	Q	F	I	W	U	U	I	I	C
D	A	A	C	U	L	L	A	U	B	S	Q	P	C	P	S	R
I	P	R	S	R	O	F	D	M	C	M	T	U	A	R	M	O
C	A	T	D	C	U	L	N	G	B	S	U	H	I	U	T	S
U	T	X	I	A	X	U	E	T	H	I	U	C	P	T	T	A
M	R	F	P	L	F	X	G	O	R	D	E	P	C	N	Y	N
P	O	D	I	U	G	N	A	L	H	I	I	N	E	U	U	C
U	C	S	S	M	N	A	V	A	R	I	C	E	C	R	S	T
Q	I	O	N	I	Y	I	P	E	R	T	U	R	B	E	C	I
K	T	M	I	S	B	V	S	U	R	R	O	G	A	T	E	F
M	Y	E	Z	K	R	E	P	A	T	R	I	A	T	I	O	N
F	A	C	S	I	M	I	L	E	Z	K	V	U	N	B	B	M

Answers on page 149.

BEST PICTURE OSCAR WINNERS

RIFF & BERNARDO LEAD 2 WARRING GANGS IN NEW YORK CITY IN THIS 1961 MUSICAL	WHAT IS ____?
IN 2011 JEAN DUJARDIN WAS A MAN OF FEW WORDS IN THIS BLACK & WHITE FILM	WHAT IS ____?
THE TITLE OF THIS 2014 BEST PICTURE REFERS TO A SUPERHERO THAT MICHAEL KEATON ONCE PLAYED	WHAT IS ____?
RUSSELL CROWE SWINGS HIS SWORD IN THIS 2000 DRAMA	WHAT IS ____?
IN THIS 1986 WINNER CHARLIE SHEEN DISCOVERS THAT WAR IS HELL	WHAT IS ____?

ACROSS

1 ACCESS ONTO THE HIGHWAY
5 4TH AND LONG PLAY, OFTEN
9 NOTHING, SOUTH OF THE BORDER
13 COUNTESS'S SPOUSE
14 CRAZY WAY TO RUN
15 BROTHER OF SNEEZY
16
18 FLORIDA LIZARD
19 NOT A SINGLE PERSON
20 SPORTS DRINK SUFFIX, PERHAPS
21 SIT OUT THE VOTE
24
28 GROOMS FEATHERS
29 ET ___ (AND OTHERS): LAT.
30 BRAIN AND SPINAL CORD: ABBR.
31 ALASKA OR OKLA., ONCE
32 OPERA HIGHLIGHTS

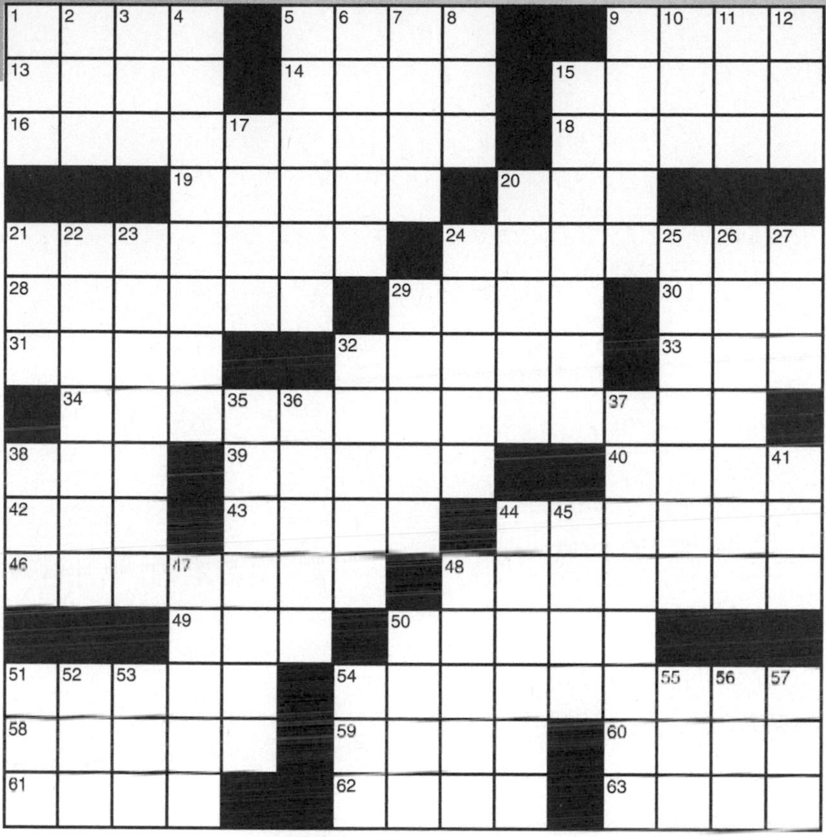

33 EARLY NUCLEAR ORG.
34
38 PART OF AN ID
39 DEVIL'S DOMAIN
40 PALE BLUE HUE
42 OZARK ___ OF COMICS
43 TEHERAN'S COUNTRY
44 JOURNALIST ALEXANDER AND OTHERS
46
48 READY-MADE COMPUTER GRAPHICS
49 "SON OF" IN ARABIC NAMES
50 LOOSE-FITTING DRESS
51 VENICE "STREET"
54
58 "SKYFALL" VOCALIST
59 "THE BACHELOR" PROP
60 ANEMIC ONE'S NEED
61 POINTILLIST'S POINTS
62 GETS A GLIMPSE OF
63 CALIF. WINE VALLEY

DOWN

1 ABBR. FOR A PROFESSOR EMERITUS
2 "FEELS SO GOOD!"
3 DESERT STORM CHOW, BRIEFLY
4 SNACK BRAND WITH A MONOCLED MASCOT
5 CREOLE, E.G.
6 GOLDEN GOPHERS' SCH.
7 CYRANO'S FAMOUS FEATURE
8 BOX OFFICE PURCHASE, FOR SHORT
9 NINE-PIECE BAND
10 ABBR. ON MAIL TO A SOLDIER
11 ACTOR BENICIO ___ TORO
12 SAILOR'S AFFIRMATIVE
15 ARP OR DUCHAMP
17 BROWN-AND-WHITE HORSE
20 WORD ON A WANTED POSTER
21 WELL PUT
22 COLD ONE, SLANGILY
23 MORE TRANQUIL
24 CARRIES ON, AS A TRADE
25 MUSICAL "SWEET POTATO"
26 COMMON LEASE SPAN
27 HUSH-HUSH GROUP THAT ADVISES THE PRES.
29 FOREST IN "AS YOU LIKE IT"
32 QUINN OF "ELEMENTARY"
35 SEWER'S PROTECTION
36 WRAP BRAND
37 WHITMAN'S POETIC REFERENCE TO ABRAHAM LINCOLN
38 LISA TO BART OR VICE VERSA
41 WWII LANDING CRAFT
44 PLAYGROUND FAVORITES
45 STEREO SYSTEM OF YORE
47 USES A ROTARY PHONE
48 RUN IN PURSUIT OF
50 WORD WITH -EYED OR GIN
51 BOUNDER
52 COMMOTION
53 AMOUNT AFTER COSTS
54 CANINE SOUNDS
55 SINGER'S NONSENSE SYLLABLE
56 ALLEY ___ (BASKETBALL MANEUVER)
57 GENETIC "MESSENGER"

Answers on page 150.

HEALTH AND MEDICINE

USED TO DIAGNOSE THINGS LIKE MENINGITIS, A LUMBAR PUNCTURE IS ALSO CALLED THIS	WHAT IS ____?
OF THE 3 COMMON TYPES OF BURN, THIS INTERMEDIATE TYPE IS TYPIFIED BY BLISTERS & SWELLING	WHAT IS ____?
VERY SIMPLY, MYALGIA IS PAIN IN ANY ONE OF THESE, OFTEN DUE TO A STRESS INJURY	WHAT IS ____?
HEPATITIS, WHICH CAN BE SEVERE OR CAUSE NO SYMPTOMS AT ALL, IS AN INFLAMMATION OF THIS ORGAN	WHAT IS ____?
A.L.S., THE MOST COMMON FORM OF MOTOR NEURON DISEASE, IS ALSO NAMED FOR THIS MAN	WHO IS ____?

ADIPOSE
ALBINISM
ALLERGEN
ANEURYSM
ANGIOPLASTY
CHEMOTHERAPY
DELIRIUM
DELTA WAVES
DERMIS
DIURETIC
ENDOCRINE
HEMATOMA
HOMEOSTASIS
KERATIN
KETOSIS

MACROPHAGE
METABOLISM
PSYCHOGENIC
RENAL
ROSACEA
SCIATICA
URETHRA
UVULA
VENULES

E	D	E	L	T	A	W	A	V	E	S	E	D	E	E	M	C
E	G	A	H	P	O	R	C	A	M	D	F	G	M	S	L	I
W	D	L	E	Y	L	U	R	E	T	H	R	A	L	I	O	S
V	I	U	C	M	T	N	I	T	A	R	F	K	V	M	U	E
E	U	V	H	U	E	S	O	P	I	D	A	E	E	R	G	C
N	R	U	E	S	Q	E	A	R	X	S	R	S	N	E	E	O
U	E	G	M	C	J	X	O	L	P	I	A	C	D	D	H	N
L	T	J	O	L	S	S	B	I	P	S	L	I	O	I	R	D
E	I	B	T	E	A	L	N	G	Y	O	B	N	C	A	I	D
S	C	Z	H	C	E	A	U	H	M	T	I	E	R	M	G	E
L	K	R	E	A	L	L	E	R	G	E	N	G	I	O	F	G
K	G	A	R	T	I	S	H	S	Y	K	I	O	N	T	B	R
M	E	T	A	B	O	L	I	S	M	T	S	H	E	A	R	E
X	X	P	P	A	N	E	U	R	Y	S	M	C	M	M	E	E
E	M	O	Y	D	E	L	I	R	I	U	M	Y	M	E	N	X
K	I	T	Q	S	C	I	A	T	I	C	A	S	P	H	A	A
B	S	I	S	A	T	S	O	E	M	O	H	P	Q	W	L	V

Answers on page 150.

IN SAN FRANCISCO

AT MARKET & POWELL STREETS, YOU'LL FIND THE SOUTHERN TURNTABLE FOR THESE CONVEYANCES	WHAT ARE ____?
THE GIANTS' HOME BASE IS AT 24 THIS PLAZA NAMED FOR THE BELOVED NO. 24	WHAT IS ____?
THE 1960s HOME OF THE GRATEFUL DEAD WAS 710 THIS STREET, NEAR THE INTERSECTION WITH HAIGHT	WHAT IS ____?
A SECTION OF THIS ROAD ON RUSSIAN HILL MAKES IT ONE OF THE "CROOKEDEST" IN THE WORLD	WHAT IS ____?
IN A 1990 THRILLER MICHAEL KEATON MOVES INTO THESE "HEIGHTS", AN AREA KNOWN FOR ITS VICTORIAN HOMES	WHAT IS ____?

AMOEBA
BART
CHINA BEACH
COIT TOWER
COLE VALLEY
DOELGER CITY
FORT FUNSTON
FORT MASON
INDIA BASIN
LAKE MERCED
LEVI'S PLAZA
MISSION BAY
NOB HILL
OCEAN BEACH
PAINTED LADIES

PIER 39
RUSSIAN HILL
SUTRO BATHS

S	Y	A	M	E	I	L	L	I	W	G	G	W	G	J	S	Z
C	H	F	O	R	T	F	U	N	S	T	O	N	F	P	F	S
L	O	C	T	T	E	E	R	T	S	Y	R	U	B	H	S	A
S	L	L	O	M	B	A	R	D	S	T	R	E	E	T	E	J
H	D	I	E	I	N	I	S	A	B	A	I	D	N	I	I	P
T	E	L	H	V	T	F	D	B	G	O	F	I	C	Z	D	P
A	C	L	H	B	A	T	S	P	C	N	9	A	T	S	A	V
B	R	I	C	Q	O	L	O	P	W	3	B	I	Y	C	L	A
O	E	H	A	E	W	N	L	W	R	L	X	W	I	K	D	B
R	M	N	E	I	F	G	U	E	E	B	O	F	V	N	E	E
T	E	A	B	Y	S	A	I	C	Y	R	I	Z	C	F	T	O
U	K	I	A	Z	V	P	A	R	E	C	V	I	C	Y	N	M
S	A	S	N	F	O	R	T	M	A	S	O	N	S	K	I	A
G	L	S	I	B	S	L	E	V	I	S	P	L	A	Z	A	S
A	H	U	H	C	A	E	B	N	A	E	C	O	H	N	P	T
E	B	R	C	W	D	R	M	I	S	S	I	O	N	B	A	Y
O	E	X	S	I	H	Y	T	I	C	R	E	G	L	E	O	D

Answers on page 150.

BROADWAY MUSICALS BY SONGS

SKY MASTERSON & THE CRAP SHOOTERS: "LUCK BE A LADY"	WHAT IS ____?
MISS HANNIGAN: "LITTLE GIRLS"	WHAT IS ____?
THE FULL COMPANY: "JUST LIKE PARADISE" & "NOTHIN' BUT A GOOD TIME"	WHAT IS ____?
CURLY & LAUREY: "PEOPLE WILL SAY WE'RE IN LOVE"	WHAT IS ____?
THE ROYAL CHILDREN: "MARCH OF THE SIAMESE CHILDREN"	WHAT IS ____?

ACROSS

1 LINE IN A SONG
6 EGYPTIAN SACRED BIRD
10 "YUK, YUK" KIN
14 BRITISH POP SINGER LEWIS
15 BARNES & NOBLE E-READER
16 PORTENTOUS EVENT
17 HACKNEYED
18 "BELOVED" NOVELIST MORRISON
19 "___LANGUAGE": 1993 BEST-SELLER
20 H.S. YEARBOOK BUYERS
21
24 CITY THAT SYMBOLIZES MIDDLE AMERICA
25 DEAL WITH A KNOT
26 JAPANESE GRILL
29 BREAD SERVED IN AN INDIAN CAFE
31

33 INTELLIGENCE, SLANGILY
37 CORDELIA'S FATHER
38 NAVIGATION AID, FOR SHORT
40 MINE FIND
41 AMOUNT IN A BRYLCREEM SLOGAN
42 NATIVE-BORN ISRAELI
45 ADORABLE ONE
47 WORD REPEATED BEFORE "TEKEL, UPHARSIN"
48 SATIRIZE
50
54 EXAMS FOR FUTURE ATTYS.
55 SPEED WAGONS OF OLD AUTODOM
56 ENCYCLOPEDIA BROWN JOB
60 ALLEY OOP'S LOVE
61
63 UNIQUE PERSON, IN OLD SLANG
64 CARTOON GIRL WITH A TALKING BACKPACK
65 BEDSIDE BUZZER
66 BOOT-CAMP CUISINE
67 TAN AND SCHUMER
68 BRIEF AND TO THE POINT

DOWN

1 LAWYERS' DEGREES
2 DATE ON A PENNY
3 HOWARD AND JAWORSKI
4 LIGHTNING ___ BOTTLE
5 W. COAST ENGINEERING SCHOOL
6 TEMPORARY PERIOD
7 FIRST IN A MULTI-VOLUME SET
8 SEA BETWEEN GREECE AND ITALY
9 IT'S ALL AROUND YOU
10 HALLELUJAH KIN
11 BOTANICAL SPIKE (OR PEARL JAM BASSIST JEFF)
12 FICTIONAL ALPINE MISS
13
22 CHOCOLATE SNACK THAT'S GOOD FOR A LAUGH?
23 AMERICAN TERRITORY IN THE PACIFIC
24 EARLY "TONIGHT" SHOW HOST JACK
26 HAMMERLOCK OR FULL NELSON
27 BIG NAME IN DO-IT-YOURSELF FURNITURE
28 BE A TATTLER
30 BALAAM S BEAST
32 CABINET DEPT. CONCERNED WITH FARMING
34 FORMER NEWSPAPER SECTION FOR SHORT
35 DESTINY'S CHILD WAS ONE
36 NOT OUT OF VIEW
39 INEPT BOXERS, IN SLANG
42 CORAL AND CHINA
43 "BARBARA ___" (BEACH BOYS HIT)
44 BOUDOIR
45 950, IN OLD ROME
46 LIKE RODEO DRIVE SHOPS
47 SOME RED DWARFS
49 "AND FURTHERMORE..."
50 EUPHORIA'S OPPOSITE
51 MAINE-TO-FLORIDA HWY.
52 SOME LOCKS
53 EXPRESS DISAPPROVAL OF
57 CULTURE MEDIUM
58 SUN. TALKS
59 GIRL IN A SALINGER STORY
61 ABBR. ON A VITAMIN BOTTLE
62 HAVING A SPARE TIRE, MAYBE

Answers on page 151.

WORDS FOUND INSIDE "INFORMATION"

A FLAT BOAT MADE BY TYING TOGETHER LONG PIECES OF WOOD	WHAT IS ____?
INSECT THAT CAN BE CARPENTER OR ARMY	WHAT IS ____?
IT'S A CANADIAN PROVINCE	WHAT IS ____?
THE FIRST OF ISAAC NEWTON'S 3 LAWS OF THIS IS THE LAW OF INERTIA	WHAT IS ____?
TO SWOON	WHAT IS ____?

AFOOT
AMINO
FIRM
FOAM
FORM
IRONMAN
MAIN
MAROON
MART
MINION
MONO
MORON
MOTOR
NATION
NONFAT

NOON
NORM
ORATION
ORION
RAIN
RANT
RATION
ROMANO

X	T	U	H	X	L	F	W	L	D	T	T	M	A	I	N	O
T	N	A	M	N	O	R	I	R	T	N	N	M	O	Y	I	I
F	M	D	G	R	N	O	I	R	O	O	I	I	O	N	N	J
A	R	T	M	R	J	N	C	I	N	N	O	Y	A	T	O	Q
R	Z	N	P	H	P	L	T	A	I	I	C	F	N	F	O	R
E	F	A	C	C	B	A	M	O	V	M	D	A	A	S	N	R
N	Y	R	Q	O	R	O	N	R	P	N	T	N	F	Q	H	B
Y	J	B	G	O	R	O	Y	T	Y	I	O	A	G	R	U	I
V	V	O	T	H	M	E	J	D	O	S	M	C	V	F	P	T
F	C	K	T	O	R	I	U	N	W	A	S	B	Q	L	R	D
T	B	C	T	A	A	J	O	I	R	A	T	N	O	A	W	A
R	F	I	T	A	N	U	N	O	R	O	M	Z	M	J	D	R
E	O	I	Z	N	O	Y	O	O	S	U	Z	N	Y	T	Y	N
N	O	F	B	I	N	N	Y	L	Z	W	C	T	L	W	N	E
N	A	T	K	A	F	N	O	R	M	R	I	F	F	F	C	W
D	C	O	V	R	A	O	N	I	M	A	E	J	W	C	V	N
R	F	B	J	C	T	S	F	O	A	M	W	Q	V	J	S	G

Answers on page 151.

LANDMARKS

TEDDY ROOSEVELT LAID THE CORNERSTONE OF ROOSEVELT ARCH, AT THE NORTH ENTRANCE OF THIS NATIONAL PARK	WHAT IS ____?
FRANK GEHRY DESIGNED THE GUGGENHEIM MUSEUM IN BILBAO IN THIS COUNTRY	WHAT IS ____?
THE STATUESQUE RESIDENTS OF THIS SOUTH PACIFIC ISLAND ARE BIG HEADED	WHAT IS ____?
A GILT STATUE OF THIS FIRE-STEALER IS AT THE HEART OF ROCKEFELLER CENTER	WHAT IS ____?
AUSTRIAN ARCHITECT ALFRED PREIS DESIGNED THE MEMORIAL OVER THIS WWII BATTLESHIP	WHAT IS ____?

ACROPOLIS
ALPS
APPALACHIA
BERLIN WALL
BIG BEN
CAPITOL HILL
COLOSSEUM
EIFFEL TOWER
FORBIDDEN CITY
GRAND CANYON
HOLLYWOOD
LONDON EYE
MACHU PICHU
NOTRE DAME
POMPEII

ST. BASIL'S
STONEHENGE
TAJ MAHAL
TIMES SQUARE
TOKYO TOWER
WILLIS TOWER

J T E R T D K V U Z E N Q L P F I C P
E D I E R L L E E M J X Y A O A X U N
L O A W E F L Y N B F A E H M P N H P
C A Y O W M D C O E O R A A P P L C R
O F H T O W U A T I R Q S M E A O I W
L E L O T L P P S F B W T J I L N P M
O G H Y S L R I W F I O E A I A D U N
S N O K I A O T O E D S R T L C O H O
S E L O L W M O L L D I I P U H N C Y
E H L T L N E L L T E L S D N I E A N
U E Y L I I T H E O N O L F T A Y M A
M N W U W L H I Y W C P A Q N K E S C
X O O C H R E L G E I O N Y G M P B D
Y T O E T E U L J R T R D J U A I F N
I S D W E B S Y L H Y C Q P I G M J A
A N O Z I R A S S U M A T N B M W T R
N L P P A W E R A U Q S S E M I T V G
E P S L I S A B T S Z T N C G R J Z O
X P H X E M A D E R T O N W L R Y D J

Answers on page 151.

CLASSIC POP LYRICS

THE BEATLES TOLD THIS TITLE GUY TO "TAKE A SAD SONG AND MAKE IT BETTER"	WHO IS ____?
JAN & DEAN SANG THAT THERE WERE "TWO GIRLS FOR EVERY BOY" HERE	WHAT IS ____?
"EVERYBODY'S TALKIN' 'BOUT THE NEW SOUND, FUNNY, BUT IT'S STILL" THIS TO BILLY JOEL	WHAT IS ____?
ABOUT HER, SIMON & GARFUNKEL SAID, "JESUS LOVES YOU MORE THAN YOU WILL KNOW, WO, WO, WO"	WHO IS ____?
IN THIS 1957 ELVIS HIT, "SPIDER MURPHY PLAYED THE TENOR SAXOPHONE"	WHAT IS ____?

ACROSS

1 KIND OF BAG OR BOARD
5 SNOOZE, IN SONORA
11 1999 FRANK MCCOURT BOOK
14 SANTA ___ (HOT CALIFORNIA WINDS)
15 LET OUT, AS FISHING LINE
16 BAND BLASTER
17
19 INITS. ON MOST ROLLING STONES RECORDS
20 ONLINE CHATS, FOR SHORT
21 BOB HOPE WAS OFTEN PART OF ONE
23 CROCKETT'S LAST BATTLE
26 "WONDER WOMAN" ACTRESS GADOT
28 "HOW STEAK IS DONE" SAUCE
29 TAKE DEAD AIM AT

31 RESPONDS BRATTILY TO
33 BUTTONLESS TOP
34 LACE AND RICKRACK
36
41 TENON'S PARTNER
42 ALWAYS, TO YEATS
44 1970S MOCEDADES HIT THAT TRANSLATES TO "IT'S YOU"
47
50
51 BOAT, TRADITIONALLY
52 COWBOY ROPE
53 PRIME EXAMPLE
56 AVERAGE GRADE
57 "___ FOR COOKIE" ("SESAME STREET" SONG)
58
64 THE WAY, IN CHINA
65 FIX, AS A SHOWER STALL
66 "HIGH SCHOOL MUSICAL" EXTRA
67 "KUNG FU" ACTOR PHILIP
68 LINE ON A WEATHER MAP
69 GRIMM HEAVY

DOWN

1 GRIZZLED SAILOR
2 MUSICIAN YOKO
3 MIDDLE OF A THREE-WORD GAME
4 ICE CREAM TREAT ___ PIE
5 BASKS ON THE BEACH
6 NEITHER DEM. NOR REP.
7 DROP THE BALL, E.G.
8 HAN RIVER CAPITAL
9 NOS. ON BUSINESS CARDS
10 FRENCH PHONE GREETING
11 CULTURAL NO-NOS
12 PROTECTED BY SHOTS, PERHAPS
13 SIGHTS AT OXFORD
18 MINE, IN PARIS
22 ITALIAN POET OF "RINALDO"
23 PIONEERING ANTI-AIDS DRUG
24 COBB OF "12 ANGRY MEN"
25 IT'S FIGURED IN SQUARE FEET
26 NO-SHOW IN A SAMUEL BECKETT PLAY
27 CAUSE OF HAND WRINGING
30 FIRST PRIME MINISTER OF INDIA
31 LIP-CURLING LOOK
32 DEPT. THAT SPONSORS THE 4-H CLUB
35 DEBATE TOPIC
37 "NO MORE, THANKS"
38 PARCEL OF LAND
39 "PET" PLANT WITH GREEN HAIR
40 ETTA OF OLD COMICS
43 SCANDINAVIAN RUG TYPE
44 VOLCANIC SPEWINGS
45 INDONESIA'S BASIC CURRENCY UNIT
46 STOCK-TICKER INVENTOR
48 GRATIS, TO GRETEL
49 HUNDRED, IN HONDURAS
51 SIXTH, IN ITALY
54 BIBLICAL KING OR ACTOR KATZ
55 GI'S VITTLES
56 "GOOD BUDDY" ON THE ROAD
59 BBQ MORSEL
60 CRAY OR GRAN ENDER
61 PART OF A CIRC.
62 "... ___ THE FIELDS WE GO"
63 L.A.-TO-LAS VEGAS DIR.

Answers on page 152.

NATIONAL PARKS A–Z

A: THIS UTAH PARK THAT HAS THE NATURAL SANDSTONE FORMATIONS IN ITS NAME, PLUS THE FIERY FURNACE	WHAT IS ____?
B: THIS PARK IN SOUTH DAKOTA WHOSE NAME REFERS TO THE DIFFICULTY OF TRAVERSING ITS RUGGED TERRAIN	WHAT IS ____?
G: THIS ARIZONA NATIONAL PARK THAT'S ALSO A UNESCO WORLD HERITAGE SITE	WHAT IS ____?
S: WHAT IS NOW THIS CALIFORNIA NATIONAL PARK WAS ESTABLISHED IN 1890 TO PROTECT A GROVE OF BIG TREES	WHAT IS ____?
Z: IT'S THE ONLY NATIONAL PARK THAT FITS THE BILL	WHAT IS ____?

ACADIA
BIG BEND
BISCAYNE
BRYCE CANYON
CAPITOL REEF
CRATER LAKE
EVERGLADES
GLACIER
GRAND TETON
HOT SPRINGS
JOSHUA TREE
KINGS CANYON
MAMMOTH CAVE
MESA VERDE
OLYMPIC

PINNACLES
SHENANDOAH
WIND CAVE

YELLOWSTONE
YOSEMITE

V	S	G	N	I	R	P	S	T	O	H	G	B	U	R	M	L
H	X	H	B	R	Y	C	E	C	A	N	Y	O	N	H	R	E
V	N	F	E	X	R	B	A	D	L	A	N	D	S	S	K	M
C	O	S	B	N	F	E	E	R	L	O	T	I	P	A	C	A
I	Y	E	I	O	A	W	U	D	W	E	E	R	L	J	C	E
P	N	V	S	Y	M	N	I	Z	R	N	Q	R	D	A	Y	J
M	A	A	C	N	E	B	D	N	X	G	E	K	D	E	E	C
Y	C	C	A	A	S	V	K	O	D	T	Z	I	O	N	N	P
L	D	H	Y	C	A	G	E	B	A	C	A	O	Q	R	O	I
O	N	T	N	S	V	R	L	R	I	H	A	P	U	Z	T	N
A	A	O	E	G	E	Q	C	A	G	G	B	V	K	I	S	N
E	R	M	U	N	R	Q	S	H	C	L	B	R	E	E	W	A
C	G	M	K	I	D	K	U	Z	E	I	A	E	E	J	O	C
D	S	A	V	K	E	Z	H	O	X	S	E	D	N	M	L	L
G	F	M	T	Y	O	S	E	M	I	T	E	R	E	D	L	E
J	O	S	H	U	A	T	R	E	E	A	B	W	R	S	E	S
G	R	A	N	D	T	E	T	O	N	G	W	Z	M	C	Y	N

Answers on page 152.

ANCIENT EMPIRES

THE PEOPLE OF THIS EMPIRE CALLED THEMSELVES THE MEXICA OR TENOCHCA	WHO ARE ____?
THE GREAT-GREAT-GRANDSON OF AUGUSTUS, HE STARTED FIDDLING AROUND AS ROMAN EMPEROR IN 54 A.D.	WHO IS ____?
THE BYZANTINES PAID TRIBUTES OF GOLD TO THIS BIG BAD HUN WHO ATTACKED THEM REPEATEDLY IN THE 440s	WHO IS ____?
AT THE TIME OF HIS DEATH IN 1227, HIS MONGOL EMPIRE STRETCHED FROM BEIJING TO THE CASPIAN SEA	WHO IS ____?
IN 1326 THE OTTOMANS MOVED THEIR CAPITAL TO BURSA, WHICH IS IN THIS ASIAN PART OF MODERN-DAY TURKEY	WHAT IS ____?

AKKADIANS
ALEXANDRIA
ASSYRIA
BABYLON
BYZANTINE
EGYPT
GREECE
GUPTA
HAMMURABI
HITTITES
INCAS
MACEDONIA
MAYANS
MESOPOTAMIA
OTTOMANS

ROME
SONG DYNASTY
SUMER
TENOCHTITLAN
ZULU

H	A	M	M	U	R	A	B	I	K	A	J	V	V	U	Q	U
G	E	N	G	H	I	S	K	H	A	N	S	E	T	V	H	L
S	N	A	M	O	T	T	O	Y	U	Q	X	S	C	Y	F	U
P	Y	O	S	M	A	N	K	H	T	R	E	S	Y	M	T	Z
A	K	F	Z	X	T	M	A	Y	A	N	S	C	Q	R	C	E
H	J	A	L	A	P	W	P	I	P	Y	Q	A	E	E	I	P
X	F	A	Y	K	U	V	L	H	N	W	R	E	T	E	O	A
K	P	I	S	E	G	P	M	D	C	C	O	Z	R	I	R	K
S	O	N	G	D	Y	N	A	S	T	Y	A	V	E	E	L	G
I	B	O	I	A	K	K	A	D	I	A	N	S	M	V	E	U
Q	A	D	L	N	L	Q	H	W	V	G	F	T	U	E	M	S
P	B	E	H	A	A	I	M	A	T	O	P	O	S	E	M	G
Z	Y	C	C	T	B	V	T	S	E	T	I	T	T	I	H	V
I	L	A	E	O	N	A	L	T	I	T	H	C	O	N	E	T
R	O	M	E	L	A	L	E	X	A	N	D	R	I	A	I	V
X	N	X	K	I	F	T	P	Y	G	E	T	H	Q	W	U	Z
L	B	Y	Z	A	N	T	I	N	E	V	N	E	R	O	G	Z

Answers on page 152.

COOKING "P"s

THE NAME OF THIS TUBULAR PASTA IS FROM THE ITALIAN FOR "QUILL"; YOU CAN PREPARE IT "ALLA VODKA"	WHAT IS ____?
THE CONSISTENCY OF THIS HAWAIIAN FINGER FOOD RANGES FROM "1-FINGER" TO "3-FINGER" IN THICKNESS	WHAT IS ____?
TO IMMERSE FOOD, OFTEN VEGGIES, FOR A BRIEF TIME IN 212-DEGREE WATER	WHAT IS ____?
IT'S THE TRADITIONAL ITALIAN PREPARATION OF A PORRIDGE MADE FROM A VARIETY OF COARSE GRAINS	WHAT IS ____?
THIS VIETNAMESE NOODLE DISH OF MEAT & RICE NOODLES IS SERVED IN A BOWL OF BEEF BROTH & SEASONINGS	WHAT IS ____?

ACROSS

1 CAPTAINS' JOURNALS
5 MAKE WATERTIGHT, IN A WAY
10 TABULA ___ (BLANK SLATE)
14 FLITTED TO A PERCH
15 CALCUTTA COIN
16 DISNEY'S "___ AND THE DETECTIVES"
17 NOT MUCH MORE THAN
18 PYROMANIAC'S ACT
19 TAPIOCA RELATIVE
20
22
23 PREPARE, AS POTATOES
24 LONGTIME INDIAN PRIME MINISTER
26 CLIMBED, AS A MOUNTAIN
29 PUFFED MUFFIN
31 WALKED IN ANKLE-DEEP WATER, SAY
32 DUSTY AND DRY

33 FAIR LADY OF CAMELOT
35 BEFORE THIS TIME
36 SNEAKY PLOTS
39 CAGEY
40 SOME HAND SANITIZERS
42 TEARS ROUGHLY
43 HOW "GREAT MINDS THINK"
45 BECOMES MORE PROFOUND
47 NILE WADERS
48 STORES AWAY
49 BUD SUPPORTER
50 SAGUAROS AND SUCH
52
56 S-SHAPED MOLDING
57 WORD BEFORE "ACETATE" OR "ALCOHOL"
60 WORD ENDING A THREAT
61 MR. PEANUT PROP
62 NEW ZEALAND NATIVE
63 MESSY BARBECUE FOOD
64 LIBERAL ___ DEGREE
65 SEATTLE HOOPSTER, FOR SHORT
66 ABOUT HALF OF ALL OFF-SPRING

DOWN

1 ALADDIN'S FIND
2 TOAST TOPPER
3 "THE ___ WITH THE DRAGON TATTOO"
4 VILLAGE SKYLINE SIGHT
5 PACKED, AS IN A BOX
6 HEARING-RELATED
7 HAPPY TIMES
8 ZODIAC'S LION
9 WRITER KESEY OR FOLLETT
10 PUT ASIDE
11 SECRETARY OR STENO
12 WRITE ON THE DOTTED LINE
13 SUCCULENT USED AS A BURN TREATMENT
21 FOOD AND WATER, FOR TWO
22
24 SOCIAL STANDARDS
25 RAPIER WITH A GUARDED TIP
26 GOODIE BAG FILLER
27 CONFINED, AS A CANARY
28 "CATCHER IN THE RYE" READ-ER, OFTEN
29 CHICK'S CHIRPS
30 GERMAN POET RAINER MA-RIA ___
32 THESE GET KICKED IN SOC-CER
34 TINTING AGENTS
37 WORK GROUP
38 SINGLE-EDGE SWORD
41 LIVING ROOM BENCHES
44 LOOSENS (UP)
46
47 SLANTED, AS TYPE
49 "HEIDI" AUTHOR JOHANNA
50 COLA OPENER
51 PETRI DISH MEDIUM
53 DISH WITH SOME OF THIS AND SOME OF THAT
54 BOOK'S ID
55 M. SCOTT PECK'S "THE ROAD ___ TRAVELED"
57 PRINTER'S DASHES
58 LAO-TZU'S "WAY"
59 RELATIVE OF SWEETIE

Answers on page 153.

PLANES, TRAINS, AND AUTOMOBILES

YOU CAN SUPPORT TRAIN TRAVEL IN MONOPOLY WHEN YOU CHANCE TO "TAKE A RIDE ON" THIS RAILROAD	WHAT IS ____?
THE SILVER CLOUD & THE SILVER GHOST ARE CLASSIC MODELS FROM THIS ALLITERATIVE LUXURY AUTOMAKER	WHAT IS ____?
THIS BRITISH & FRENCH FUNDED SUPERSONIC TRANSPORT MADE ITS LAST FLIGHTS IN 2003	WHAT IS ____?
PULLMAN'S "DELMONICO" BECAME THE FIRST TYPE OF THIS RAILROAD CAR IN 1868	WHAT IS ____?
IN 1967 THE DOUGLAS AIRCRAFT COMPANY MERGED WITH THIS AIRCRAFT COMPANY	WHAT IS ____?

AIR BAGS
BOEING
BOGIE
CHRYSLER
CONDUCTOR
DIESEL
EXHAUST
FLIGHT DATA
FORD
FREIGHT
FUSELAGE
HANGAR
HEADLIGHTS
HYBRID
MAGLEV

MONOREAIL

NEUTRAL

PILOT

SUV

TARMAC

TRUCK

WINDSHIELD

WINGS

D	I	N	I	N	G	C	A	R	K	H	S	Y	V	T	E	Q
W	P	D	G	T	T	A	R	M	A	C	H	Y	B	R	I	D
L	B	I	R	I	H	S	D	A	W	T	G	N	I	E	O	B
H	M	U	C	O	N	D	U	C	T	O	R	B	O	G	I	E
I	C	A	C	M	E	S	H	A	A	J	R	W	I	N	G	S
K	P	R	G	L	P	B	T	U	H	P	I	L	O	T	F	E
P	H	O	C	L	U	E	C	H	I	X	O	D	I	U	D	X
V	F	L	H	E	E	V	E	U	G	K	E	A	S	R	W	M
T	U	L	R	N	D	V	P	F	G	I	N	E	O	I	O	Q
H	O	S	Y	N	I	R	R	N	I	E	L	C	N	N	F	B
G	H	R	S	O	E	A	Q	X	U	A	N	D	O	P	S	R
I	T	O	I	D	S	G	I	T	G	O	S	R	A	G	C	E
E	K	Y	E	C	E	N	R	E	C	H	A	F	A	E	Z	A
R	Z	C	R	M	L	A	C	P	I	I	D	B	U	X	H	D
F	O	E	P	B	L	H	F	E	L	Q	R	I	N	D	U	I
G	I	V	O	X	S	Z	L	X	A	I	O	S	B	N	X	N
F	L	I	G	H	T	D	A	T	A	J	F	H	B	S	G	G

Answers on page 153.

FAMOUS AMERICANS

LEON WAGENER'S BIOGRAPHY OF HIM IS ENTITLED "ONE GIANT LEAP"	WHO IS ____?
HE WAS THE FIRST AFRICAN-AMERICAN CHAIRMAN OF THE JOINT CHIEFS OF STAFF	WHO IS ____?
"A MAGICIAN AMONG THE SPIRITS" IS A 1924 BOOK BY THIS MAN	WHO IS ____?
FROM 1935 TO 1937 SHE WORKED AT PURDUE UNIVERSITY AS A CAREER COUNSELOR & AS AN ADVISOR IN AERONAUTICS	WHO IS ____?
THIS NEW YORKER WHO FOUGHT AT THE BATTLE OF GETTYSBURG WAS ONCE CONSIDERED THE INVENTOR OF BASEBALL	WHO IS ____?

ACROSS

1 TRICKY BILLIARDS SHOT
6 WILL ROGERS PROP
11 VIETNAM WAR PROTEST GRP.
14 JAPAN'S SECOND-LARGEST CITY
15 "___ CASSIO!": OTHELLO
16 MUSEUM STUFF
17
19 LAW, IN FRANCE
20 BACKDROP FOR MUCH OF "FROZEN"
21 "DIES ___" (LATIN REQUIEM)
22 COMFORTER FILL
23
27 ATHLETIC ORG. FOR DUKE AND CLEMSON
28 SMALLER THAN SMALL
29
35 SHE, IN LISBON

36 SIGN-OFF WORD, WITH "YOURS"

37

44 BREAKS UP A SENTENCE FOR ANALYSIS

45 YELLOW FEVER MOSQUITO

47

52 VIRTUOUS ONE

54 "THERE OUGHTA BE ___!"

55 DOUBLE-CURVED MOLDING

56 SHIP'S JOURNAL

57 "GET SHORTY" NOVELIST LEONARD

59 KENTUCKY DERBY WINNER ___ RIDGE

60 BEFORE, POETICALLY

61 CIVIL WAR SIDE

62 LINGUIST-ACTIVIST CHOM-SKY

63 SCOUNDREL

64 FULL OF CHEEKY ATTITUDE

65 IRS FORM IDS

DOWN

1 COMFORTABLE SLIPPERS, FOR SHORT

2 "UNTO US ___ IS GIVEN": ISAIAH

3 STYLING SHOP

4 GARB FOR THE SLOPES

5 SUFFIX WITH ECUADOR OR CAESAR

6 "TOORA ___..." (IRISH LULLABY SYLLABLES)

7 BATTLE OF BRANDS

8 "I CALL 'EM AS I ___"

9 "REBEL WITHOUT A CAUSE" STAR MINEO

10 MAGIC, ON SCOREBOARDS

11 PUB'S COUSIN

12 OVERWHELMS AUDIBLY (WITH "OUT")

13 LIKE SCROOGE

18 INFANT'S WRAPPER WORN OVER A DIAPER

22 THREE, IN BERLIN

24 MORE THAN COLD

25 MOVIE-AD DISPLAY

26 LIKE DECADES

29 PILE, AS OF RUBBLE

30 JESSICA OF "FANTASTIC FOUR"

31 WORKED TO THE BONE

32 SIOUX TRIBESMAN

33 NEIGHBOR OF BRAZ. AND ARG.

34 NAME, AS A KNIGHT

38 SALINGER'S FOR "___— WITH LOVE AND SQUALOR"

39 FISHERMEN, AT TIMES

40 HIGH-SPEED INTERNET LETTERS

41 RENDERS HARMLESS, AS A BULL

42 SLOW BALLET DANCES

43 ARMENIA'S CAPITAL

46 PREPARES CLAMS, PERHAPS

48 POETIC FEET

49 HEALING PLANTS

50 BEFORE DAWN, PERHAPS

51 AMAZES, IN A GOOD WAY

52 BALDWIN WHO WAS JACK RYAN

53 WIFE IN "THE THIN MAN"

58 MEADOW

Answers on page 153.

POP MUSIC RHYME TIME

DOGGY DOGG'S CHICKEN HOUSES	WHAT ARE ____?
JAGGER'S BALLPOINT PENS	WHAT ARE ____?
HAGAR'S NIGHTCLOTHES	WHAT ARE ____?
MARLEY'S HIGH-ARCING TENNIS SHOTS	WHAT ARE ____?
EX-BLACK SABBATH SINGER'S MUPPET BEARS	WHAT ARE ____?

ALICE'S CHALICES
BALLAD SALAD
COBAIN'S DOMAIN
DANCIN' MANSON
DIBS ON GIBSON
DOUGHY BOWIE
DYLAN'S VILLAIN
HANK STANK
HOLLY'S FOLLIES
MOON CROONS
RINGO'S BINGO
SHOWIN' COHEN
SLAM-DUNK FUNK
STIPE'S PIPES

S S A M M Y S J A M M I E S L J N O G
P B D P K B K N F E T B N B B P X V Q
O U Z K D W N R S O K O Q A Q O P S E
O D H A A M A P I N M B M T U O C N E
C Z R N L K T W H N D S I S L Q Y O S
S T P A A C S D O Z G L F C O Q N O L
P D D L S O K O L O L O V D X P Z R A
O A Y I D B N U L S J B S I B Z X C M
O N L C A A A G Y F L S F B Y P C N D
N C A E L I H H S M I L C S I W U O U
S I N S L N N Y F Y J U F O M N W O N
H N S C A S A B O I R O C N I T G M K
A M V H B D J O L K Z B G G C H B O F
T A I A X O A W L Z Y D U I K M A N U
D N L L O M I I I A Z O N B S H P V N
Z S L I Q A O E E V G I P S B Q U E K
Q O A C H I S J S B B J A O I O B N R
C N I E G N A N S H O W I N C O H E N
S T N S T I P E S P I P E S S I Q M L

Answers on page 154.

MUSEUMS

THE AMSTERDAM HOUSE WHERE THIS DIARIST & HER FAMILY HID DURING WWII HAS BEEN A MUSEUM SINCE 1960	WHO IS ____?
THE PEABODY MUSEUM OF ARCHAEOLOGY & ETHNOLOGY IS AT THIS CAMBRIDGE, MASSACHUSETTS INSTITUTION	WHAT IS ____?
THE TATE GALLERY & THE TATE MODERN ARE IN THIS CITY	WHAT IS ____?
NEW YORK CITY HAS MANY MUSEUMS, LIKE COLUMBUS CIRCLE'S MAD, THE MUSEUM OF ARTS & THIS	WHAT IS ____?
THERE ARE MUSEUMS DEVOTED TO THIS WRITER IN KENYA & IN DENMARK	WHO IS ____?

ACROSS

1 BATHROOM RUGS
5 TIME AT A HOTEL
9 TRIPLED, IT MEANS "AND SO ON"
14 PERSIA, FORMERLY
15 "MUSIC MAN" SETTING
16 LONGTIME FILM CRITIC ROGER
17
19 LIKE A COLD SUFFERER'S VOICE
20 EDITOR'S "REMOVE IT"
21 PUT THROUGH A SIEVE
23 "___ YANKEE DOODLE DANDY"
24 "LET'S MAKE A DEAL" CHOICE
27 SPANISH DESSERT WINES
29 "MENDING WALL" POET
30 FIGS. ON SCHOOL TRANSCRIPTS

32 COLL. OR UNIV.
33 COUGAR OR JAGUAR
34 FLY LIKE A HAWK
36 NICKNAME OF LINCOLN'S YOUNGEST SON
38
42 "I ___ ROCK": SIMON AND GARFUNKEL HIT
43 GROUP FOR PEOPLE 50 AND UP
44 AVIAN PAL OF EEYORE
47 SCHOOL ZONE SIGN
50 SWEET POTATO COUSINS
52 SMIDGENS
54 COURTROOM FIGURE
56
58 TORONTO'S PROV.
59 "UNDERSTOOD!", HIPPIE-STYLE
61 "___ EVER SO HUMBLE..."
62 FORMER COLORADO SENATOR MARK
64 HEAT WAVES' OPPOSITES
68 THESAURUS COMPILER
69 TWIN WHO SOLD HIS BIRTHRIGHT
70 FLIER TO TEL AVIV
71 DAGGERS OF YORE
72 JEWISH PLACE OF WORSHIP
73 SLIGHT VERBALLY

DOWN

1 "MAMMA ___!" (BROADWAY MUSICAL)
2 PRINCE VALIANT'S FIRST SON
3 COOKED IN A CLAY OVEN, AS IN INDIA
4 SHOWS DISDAIN
5 POLICE-CAR WAILER
6 SHELLEY'S "___ SKYLARK"
7 BEARDS ON GRAIN
8 WASHINGTON CITY SOUTHEAST OF MT. RAINIER
9 1983 FILM IN WHICH BARBRA STREISAND DRESSES AS A MAN
10 "THE ___ DABA HONEYMOON"
11
12 O'NEILL WORKS, E.G.
13 "THE WAIT IS OVER!"
18 FLOATING WRECKAGE
22 SPEED DEMON'S CRY
24 MEDAL FOR AVIATORS
25 ___ PRO NOBIS (PRAY FOR US)
26 OLD-SCHOOL "OMG!"
28 RIGHT-HAND HELPER
31 LAST KING OF TROY
35 GAVE THE NOD TO
37 HAS AMBITIONS
39 CUT INTO PLANKS
40 OGDEN WHO DESCRIBED PARSLEY AS "GHARSLEY"
41 POLITE RESPONSE TO "THANK YOU"
45 ROBERT CORMIER'S "THE CHOCOLATE ___"
46 TIMOTHY LEARY'S HALLUCINOGEN
47 SCRUBS, AS POTS
48
49 UTILITY WOE
51 RESTAURANT IN A GUTHRIE SONG
53 RAMS AND LAMBS
55 DELTA DEPOSITS
57 POP SINGER PAULA
60 "GOLLY!"
63 SPIDER-MAN CREATOR STAN
65 FAMED CATCHER/BATTING INSTRUCTOR CHARLEY
66 NBA STAR ___ GASOL
67 KIND OF 35MM CAMERA, FOR SHORT

Answers on page 154.

PULITZER PRIZE WINNERS

1997 FOR BIOGRAPHY: THIS LATE AUTHOR'S "ANGELA'S ASHES"	WHO IS ____?
1923 FOR FICTION: THIS AUTHOR FOR HER NEBRASKA-SET NOVEL "ONE OF OURS"	WHO IS ____?
1945 FOR MUSIC: THIS COMPOSER FOR HIS "APPALACHIAN SPRING"	WHO IS ____?
1924 FOR POETRY: THIS NEW ENGLANDER FOR HIS "NEW HAMPSHIRE: A POEM WITH NOTES AND GRACE NOTES"	WHO IS ____?
1984 FOR DRAMA: THIS PLAYWRIGHT FOR THE THEATRICAL "GLENGARRY GLEN ROSS"	WHO IS ____?

ANNIE BAKER
ANNIE PROULX
CARL SANDBURG
CORMAC MCCARTHY
DAN FAGIN
DONNA TARTT
DOUG WRIGHT
JASON MILLER
JOHN UPDIKE
JUNOT DÍAZ
LARRY MCMURTY
PETER TAYLOR
PHILIP ROTH
RICHARD RUSSO
TONI MORRISON

W.S. MERWIN
ZOE AKINS
ZONA GALE

F	R	A	N	K	M	C	C	R	O	U	R	T	E	W	A	B
A	A	R	O	N	C	O	P	L	A	N	D	S	K	H	T	R
A	N	N	I	E	P	R	O	U	L	X	X	D	I	T	S	D
T	I	S	N	I	K	A	E	O	Z	V	H	O	D	O	O	L
N	I	W	R	E	M	S	W	O	J	N	X	U	P	R	R	D
J	C	A	R	L	S	A	N	D	B	U	R	G	U	P	F	A
U	N	D	O	N	N	A	T	A	R	T	T	W	N	I	T	N
N	R	B	E	N	G	O	Z	H	Z	F	H	R	H	L	R	F
O	T	E	M	A	M	D	I	V	A	D	T	I	O	I	E	A
T	R	E	L	L	I	M	N	O	S	A	J	G	J	H	B	G
D	P	E	T	E	R	T	A	Y	L	O	R	H	U	P	O	I
I	Y	J	A	U	W	I	L	L	A	C	A	T	H	E	R	N
A	R	E	K	A	B	E	I	N	N	A	I	Y	U	M	X	P
Z	J	T	R	J	N	O	S	I	R	R	O	M	I	N	O	T
C	O	R	M	A	C	M	C	C	A	R	T	H	Y	L	K	B
P	T	L	Z	O	S	S	U	R	D	R	A	H	C	I	R	V
J	L	A	R	R	Y	M	C	M	U	R	T	Y	I	W	N	K

Answers on page 154.

O CANADA

BY POPULATION, IT'S THE LARGEST CITY IN CANADA

WHAT IS ____?

CANADA'S 5-CENT PIECE FEATURES NOT ONLY QUEEN ELIZABETH II BUT ALSO THIS RODENT

WHAT IS ____?

THIS PROVINCE'S NAME IS THE FRENCH FORM OF AN ALGONQUIN WORD FOR "WHERE THE RIVER NARROWS"

WHAT IS ____?

CANADA DAY, JULY 1, WAS ONCE KNOWN AS THIS "DAY"

WHAT IS ____?

IT'S THE "KEYSTONE PROVINCE" BECAUSE OF ITS CENTRAL LOCATION IN THE COUNTRY

WHAT IS ____?

ACROSS

1 BASEBALL STITCHING
5 CHANNEL COVERING CAPITOL HILL
10 CHRIS OF FOOTBALL'S GIANTS
14 HEAVYWEIGHT SPORT?
15 EVOCATIVE OF YESTERYEAR
16 "OL' MAN RIVER" COMPOSER JEROME
17 "TRUE ___" (JOHN WAYNE MOVIE)
18 CATCHPHRASE OF THE '80S FROM A DIRE STRAITS SONG
20
22 SAINTLY GLOWS
23 HARNESS STRAP
24 INDONESIAN TOURIST MECCA
25
28

32 HIT ___ NOTE (HAVE A JARRING EFFECT)
33 OTTER COUSIN
34 SPOIL, AS FOOD
35 BUS. CARD NOS.
36 BOWLING ALLEYS
37 PEACE SYMBOL
38 DIFRANCO OF FOLK ROCK
39 MR. POTATO HEAD PARTS
40 FREELANCE SAMURAI
41 MICK JAGGER, FOR ONE
44 ___ DRAGON (LARGEST LIVING LIZARD)
45 KING KONG AND KIN
46 RADAR O'REILLY'S SOFT DRINK
47
50 FEATURE OF SOME WEDDING PARTIES
54 "SOUP'S ON" SUMMONER
57 ACTRESS SKYE OF "SAY ANYTHING..."
58 COST TO BE DEALT IN
59 ALL RILED UP
60 DINNER CRUMBS
61 WINE LABEL FIGURE
62 APPLE UTENSIL
63 COZY RETREAT

DOWN

1 ARMY DRILL INSTRUCTOR, OFTEN: ABBR.
2 CASH ON THE CONTINENT
3 ARAB CHIEFTAIN
4 DOUBLE-DECKER, E.G.
5 FILM REVIEWER
6 ATTACH, AS A SHIRT BUTTON
7 SCHOOL FUND-RAISING GRP.
8 SON OF VAL AND ALETA
9 POLITE DECLINE
10 LIKE MANY AN ATRIUM
11 "FINDING ___" (DISNEY FILM)
12 ART DECO DESIGNER
13 HOLDERS OF LTRS. OR BILLS
19 TIMBUKTU SETTING
21 "...AND ___ THE TWAIN SHALL MEET"
24 HARMFUL INFLUENCES
25 DOHA'S COUNTRY
26 "___ HOOKS" (SIGN ON A CRATE)
27 BORNE BY THE WIND
28 CLEMENTINE'S FATHER, BY OCCUPATION
29 DOWN EAST COLLEGE TOWN
30 OX, SHEEP OR GOAT
31 "JACK SPRAT ___ FAT"
33 THEY LIVED IN CHICHEN ITZA
36 "GO FOR IT!"
37
40 BARCELONA CHAIR DESIGNER LUDWIG MIES VAN DER ___
42 JULIE WHO VOICES MARGE SIMPSON
43 GRAF ___ (ILL-FATED GERMAN WARSHIP)
44 ASTRONOMER WHO DESCRIBED PLANETARY MOTION
46 "48 HRS." COSTAR NICK
47 CAKE-AND-CANDLES TIME, FOR SHORT
48 ONE, IN STUTTGART
49 PIER, IN ARCHITECTURE
51 INSIDE DIAMETER
52 COOKOUT INTRUDERS
53 TAKE A TIME-OUT
55 LINGERIE BUY
56 PENCIL HOLDER EVERYONE HAS

Answers on page 155.

SCRAMBLED SPORTS

A CHERRY	WHAT IS ____?
KEBAB STALL	WHAT IS ____?
MYSTIC NAGS	WHAT IS ____?
GIRL NEWTS	WHAT IS ____?
SWOONING BARD	WHAT IS ____?

BADMINTON
CLIMBING
CRICKET
DANCING
DISC GOLF
DIVING
FOOTBALL
GOLF
HANDBALL
JAI ALAI
KAYAKING
PING-PONG
SKATEBOARDING
SKIING
SOCCER

SOFTBALL
SURFING
TENNIS
UNICYCLING
VOLLEYBALL
WAKEBOARDING
WINDSURFING

H	S	C	I	T	S	A	N	M	Y	G	M	Y	R	L	U	L
B	Y	F	M	M	S	N	O	W	B	O	A	R	D	I	N	G
B	D	D	L	J	W	G	N	I	L	T	S	E	R	W	I	F
W	A	N	I	O	A	I	N	H	S	F	D	H	B	R	C	O
U	N	S	O	V	G	I	N	I	A	H	X	C	L	E	Y	O
I	C	C	K	I	I	K	A	D	F	N	L	R	K	C	C	T
S	I	N	N	E	T	N	C	L	S	R	D	A	A	C	L	B
G	N	K	S	M	T	R	G	S	A	U	U	B	Y	O	I	A
N	G	R	Q	I	I	B	H	F	V	I	R	S	A	S	N	L
I	R	U	F	C	P	V	A	E	S	D	P	F	K	L	G	L
I	P	A	K	X	P	U	S	L	I	O	O	A	I	F	L	H
K	T	E	G	N	I	B	M	I	L	C	F	P	N	N	N	S
S	T	V	O	L	L	E	Y	B	A	L	L	T	G	M	G	M
S	K	A	T	E	B	O	A	R	D	I	N	G	B	P	W	P
O	M	G	N	I	D	R	A	O	B	E	K	A	W	A	K	X
P	I	N	G	P	O	N	G	J	D	I	S	C	G	O	L	F
O	J	S	Y	V	W	B	A	D	M	I	N	T	O	N	U	L

Answers on page 155.

THANKS FOR THE MEMOIRS

IN "ON WRITING" THIS HORROR AUTHOR GAVE ADVICE TO ASPIRING WRITERS & WROTE ABOUT HIS LIFE IN MAINE	WHO IS ____?
INGRID BETANCOURT'S "EVEN SILENCE HAS AN END" RECOUNTS HER CAPTIVITY IN THE JUNGLES OF THIS COUNTRY	WHAT IS ____?
THIS MEMOIR IS SUBTITLED "ONE WOMAN'S SEARCH FOR EVERYTHING ACROSS ITALY, INDIA, AND INDONESIA"	WHAT IS ____?
"ME TALK PRETTY ONE DAY" IS A MEMOIR OF LIFE IN PARIS BY THIS HUMORIST	WHO IS ____?
BARACK OBAMA WROTE THE FOREWORD TO THIS OTHER LEADER'S BOOK "CONVERSATIONS WITH MYSELF"	WHO IS ____?

"ANGELA'S ASHES"
CHE GUEVARA
"DARKNESS VISIBLE"
"GIRL, INTERRUPTED"
"H IS FOR HAWK"
JOAN DIDION
"JUST KIDS"
"LIFE"
"LUCKY"
MARY KARR
"NIGHT"
"OUT OF AFRICA"
"THE GLASS CASTLE"
"WALDEN"
"WAVE"

S	G	N	I	K	N	E	H	P	E	T	S	K	Z	N	E	Z
I	E	F	I	L	I	U	Z	M	V	R	W	I	O	V	T	N
R	C	H	E	G	U	E	V	A	R	A	A	I	O	H	E	A
A	S	X	J	X	O	C	P	A	H	N	D	L	E	L	B	C
D	D	S	T	E	P	X	K	R	S	I	Y	G	S	D	S	I
E	I	B	Q	G	E	Y	O	Y	D	A	L	O	Q	B	K	R
S	K	W	G	R	R	F	C	N	R	A	N	T	P	S	H	F
D	T	A	C	A	S	W	A	P	S	M	W	C	X	C	L	A
I	S	L	M	I	Z	O	T	S	A	H	P	D	Y	O	X	F
V	U	D	H	O	J	A	C	N	E	V	A	W	V	L	K	O
A	J	E	R	S	E	A	D	L	P	W	I	S	O	O	Z	T
D	H	N	R	L	S	E	X	O	Q	A	E	B	I	M	L	U
R	L	O	C	T	L	E	P	X	O	X	C	G	B	B	C	O
D	L	H	L	A	F	Z	T	I	T	H	G	I	N	I	L	Q
R	S	E	H	S	A	S	A	L	E	G	N	A	O	A	Y	W
K	T	D	A	R	K	N	E	S	S	V	I	S	I	B	L	E
D	E	T	P	U	R	R	E	T	N	I	L	R	I	G	W	W

Answers on page 156.

TELEVISION

ELLEN POMPEO PLAYS ONE OF THE HEALERS IN THIS MEDICAL DRAMA

WHAT IS ____?

JOHN KRASINSKI WAS PRANKSTER JIM HALPERT ON THIS SITCOM

WHAT IS ____?

THE "H" IN "AGENTS OF S.H.I.E.L.D." STANDS FOR THIS, ALSO IN THE NAME OF A CABINET DEPARTMENT

WHAT IS ____?

THIS SHOW ABOUT A VERY OLD TIME LORD FROM THE PLANET GALLIFREY DEBUTED ON THE BBC IN 1963

WHAT IS ____?

THIS CELEB-OBSESSED SHOW GOT ITS NAME FROM A ZONE WITH A 30-MILE RADIUS USED TO MONITOR FILM SHOOTS

WHAT IS ____?

ACROSS

1 SOME HYATT EMPLOYEES
6 CAPTAIN KIDD'S HAUL
10 WIFE OF CHARLIE CHAPLIN
14 "FAREWELL, MON AMI"
15 SENIORS ORG.
16 FLIM-___ (SCAM)
17 WHAT KINGS DO ALL DAY
18
20 GOVT. FUNDS FOR THE DISABLED
21 ROD'S FISHING PARTNER
23 CLUES FOR TRACKERS
24 "THE ___ REPORT" (1976 BEST-SELLER)
25 THEY MAY BE PREPOSITIONAL
27
31 EGGNOG TOPPER
32 ADDITION TOTALS
33 STAT FOR A QB
36 "UNTO US ___ IS GIVEN":

ISAIAH
37 GOLFER ELS
39 THE EURO REPLACED IT IN ITALY
40 GYMNAST'S PERFECT SCORE
41 LAKE NEAR BUFFALO
42 TOTAL SQUARE, IN DATED SLANG
44 FOUNTAIN ORDER
46 "YIKES!"
49 SPANISH ONES
50 "FUNNY FACE" DIRECTOR STANLEY
51 CHURCH CALENDAR
52
55
58 NEVADA RESORT LAKE
60 "LA BAMBA" STAR MORALES
61 FARM PRODUCE
62 WORD WITH CUISINE OR COUTURE
63 TAKE A SIESTA
64 WIMBLEDON LEGEND ARTHUR
65 WISE ONES

DOWN

1 WHERE THE CURIOSITY ROVER ROVES
2 SUMMER THIRST QUENCHERS
3 OLD SUNDIAL NUMERAL
4 MBA OR MD, E.G.
5 IT MAY BRIGHTEN YOUR MORNING
6 SHINY COTTON FABRIC
7 KEN OF TV'S "WISEGUY"
8 "___ YOU LONESOME TONIGHT?" (ELVIS TUNE)
9 FED. DOCUMENTS PRODUCER
10 WHEN NOTHING SEEMS TO GO RIGHT
11 MIXTURES OR MEDLEYS
12 PEARLY SHELL LAYER
13 MAKE ___ OF (BOTCH)
19 PAPERWORK TO FILL OUT
22 KNICKKNACK CABINETS
24 SACRED SONG
25 SEED SPITTING NOISE
26
27 TINY PEST
28 TROJAN HORSE, E.G.
29 SCHOOL WITH FAMOUS PLAYING FIELDS
30 LOU GRANT PORTRAYER ED
33 DIGITAL RECORDING DEVICE
34 SUPREME COURT'S ___ SCOTT CASE
35 YEMEN'S CAPITAL
38 LIKE BILL GATES
39 WHAT TO EAT TO LOSE WEIGHT
41 ___ LODGE (BUDGET MOTEL)
43 USES A SANDER ON
44 "UNDERSTOOD!"
45 WHERE FRANCE IS
46 MORE UNUSUAL
47 YELLOWSTONE GRAZER
48 OLD PERUVIANS
51 "HERE COMES TROUBLE!"
52 HENCHMAN
53 SPECK OF DUST
54 SLEEP SYMBOLS
56 "HIS MASTER'S VOICE" LABEL
57 TARGETS FOR QBS
59 U.S. MOTORISTS' CLUB

Answers on page 156.

THEATER

IT'S THE MUSICAL IN WHICH FANTINE SINGS "I DREAMED A DREAM"	WHAT IS ____?
THIS JONATHAN LARSON MUSICAL WAS LOOSELY BASED ON THE OPERA "LA BOHEME"	WHAT IS ____?
IN ACT 3 OF "PYGMALION" THIS CHARACTER IS MISTAKEN FOR A HUNGARIAN PRINCESS	WHO IS ____?
EVERYONE ON STAGE IS A SUSPECT IN THE MUSICAL BASED ON DICKENS' UNFINISHED TALE "THE MYSTERY OF" HIM	WHO IS ____?
"THE LARAMIE PROJECT" IS A DOCUDRAMA-STYLE PLAY ABOUT THE 1998 MURDER OF THIS GAY COLLEGE STUDENT	WHO IS ____?

"ANGELS IN AMERICA"
"BUS STOP"
"CLOSER"
COLM TÓIBÍN
DAVID MAMET
"ELECTRA"
EUGENE O'NEILL
FLORIAN ZELLER
GORE VIDAL
"M. BUTTERFLY"
"RAISIN IN THE SUN"
SAMUEL BECKETT
SARAH RUHL
SIMON GRAY
SOPHOCLES

"VENUS IN FUR"
"WAR HORSE"
WILLIAM INGE

Y	J	Z	H	Y	L	F	R	E	T	T	U	B	M	Z	X	A
D	A	V	I	D	M	A	M	E	T	B	G	W	K	O	R	C
P	S	L	G	O	R	E	V	I	D	A	L	D	I	I	E	I
A	R	T	C	E	L	E	S	A	R	A	H	R	U	H	L	R
S	E	L	B	A	R	E	S	I	M	S	E	L	W	L	L	E
E	W	E	U	G	E	N	E	O	N	E	I	L	L	H	E	M
S	E	L	I	Z	A	D	O	O	L	I	T	T	L	E	Z	A
R	S	O	P	H	O	C	L	E	S	C	V	K	F	Y	N	N
O	S	A	M	U	E	L	B	E	C	K	E	T	T	Q	A	I
H	T	Y	O	B	I	F	K	Y	A	R	G	N	O	M	I	S
R	W	I	L	L	I	A	M	I	N	G	E	V	A	F	R	L
A	X	V	E	N	U	S	I	N	F	U	R	N	Y	R	O	E
W	M	A	T	T	H	E	W	S	H	E	P	A	R	D	L	G
P	O	T	S	S	U	B	Z	K	N	J	F	T	T	M	F	N
R	A	I	S	I	N	I	N	T	H	E	S	U	N	P	B	A
H	W	N	V	R	C	O	L	M	T	O	I	B	I	N	Q	E
D	J	I	S	K	K	D	O	O	R	D	N	I	W	D	E	T

Answers on page 157.

VIVA MEXICO!

AS A COLONY OF THAT COUNTRY, FROM 1521 TO 1821 MEXICO WAS KNOWN AS NEW THIS	WHAT IS ____?
MEXICO'S PRESIDENT FROM 2000 TO 2006, HE HAD FORMERLY BEEN PRESIDENT OF COCA COLA DE MEXICO	WHO IS ____?
THE VERTICAL STRIPES ON MEXICO'S FLAG ARE RED, WHITE & THIS COLOR	WHAT IS ____?
MEXICO CELEBRATES LABOR DAY ON THE SAME DATE AS MANY EUROPEAN NATIONS & THIS HOLIDAY 4 DAYS LATER	WHAT IS ____?
THIS ARCHDUKE OF AUSTRIA WHO BECAME EMPEROR OF MEXICO DIED BEFORE A FIRING SQUAD IN 1867	WHO IS ____?

BANDA
CALAKMUL
CAMPECHE
CORRIDOS
HERMOSILLO
MARIACHI
MONTE ALBÁN
MONTERREY
NUEVO LEON
OAXACA
PRE-COLUMBIAN
RANCHERA
SONORA
TELEMEX
UXMAL

VERACRUZ
YUCATÁN
ZAPOTEC

A C O R R I D O S H I C Y X R Z I
R C A L A K M U L O E O Q X M C Q
O M W R Q Q M O N T E R R E Y G D
N N Y D P R E C O L U M B I A N Z
O U U Y X N P P K F B V G R E E N
S E U E F D A H C I R A G T D T R
X V Y X B Z D B O H T H N A Q Z X
O O X V M Q K N L C I L G D N J R
F L N E A A O A L A A C A X A O A
E E C R X G L T I I E P A W Q R T
T O T A I R E A S R E T H N E E S
N N E C M A M C O A S Y N H E P H
E A L R I P C U M M K W C O A W K
C M E U L K E Y R I M N W I M J T
N Q M Z I F A C E X A M N S X W C
I B E F A H F V H R N Z G W O V F
V F X Q N O Y A M E D O C N I C F

Answers on page 157.

THE BODY HUMAN

Clue	Response
THE SARTORIUS IS THE BODY'S LONGEST ONE OF THESE	WHAT IS ____?
THIS SUBSTANCE THAT COVERS THE TOOTH IS THE HARDEST TISSUE IN THE BODY	WHAT IS ____?
ITS 3 MAIN SECTIONS ARE THE DUODENUM, THE JEJUNUM & THE ILEUM	WHAT IS ____?
CUSPIDS ARE ANOTHER NAME FOR THESE TEETH THAT TEAR & SHRED FOOD	WHAT ARE ____?
THIS FLAP OF CARTILAGE PREVENTS FOOD & FLUIDS FROM ENTERING YOUR WINDPIPE	WHAT IS ____?

ACROSS

1 "LADY" OF POP
5 "I LOVE YOU," IN ROME
10 DAIQUIRI BASE
13 SPACE PIONEER SHEPARD
14 WORDS WITH "THERE" AND "THE BALANCE"
15 UNRETURNED SERVE
16 DRAW OR PAINT
17 TV PAL OF JERRY AND GEORGE
18 WEB ADDRESS ELEMENT
19
22 WIND-SHELTERED
23 INVERSE TRIG FUNCTION
24 "IT'S CHILLY OUT HERE!"
26 WASHINGTONS IN THE WALLET
29 THUMBS-UP IN HOUSTON
30 USE A HARVESTER
32

37 TENNYSON POEM, E.G.
39 SIMILE CONNECTOR
40 DICKENSIAN "FIDDLESTICKS!"
41 DECORATIVE INLAID WORK
43 MCGRAW OF COUNTRY
45 ORSON WELLES' "CITIZEN"
46 UNCLUTTER
49 MONOGRAM OF OLD POSSUM'S CREATOR
50 UNDER-THE-SINK ITEM
52 USES A STRAW, PERHAPS
54 FODDER CONTAINER
55 IMMUNE SYSTEM VIRUS-FIGHTERS
57 MENTION AS AN AFTERTHOUGHT
58
60 ISN'T WELL
62 COSMO, FOR EXAMPLE
63 SIGNIFY
64 CORP. MONEY MGRS.
65 POETIC "PREVIOUSLY"
66 RED GIANT IN THE NIGHT SKY
67 BRAIN SCANS, FOR SHORT

DOWN

1 WHAT A GUY NEEDS AT THE HOEDOWN
2 BOXERS MUHAMMAD AND LAILA
3 THEY GAVE THE HULK HIS POWERS
4 YEAR'S RECORD
5 ANKLEBONES
6 "BACK ___ HOUR" (SHOP SIGN)
7 ANTACID TARGET
8 DIAMOND OR QUARTZ
9 MODEST ICE CREAM ORDER
10 WHEEL SPOKES, GEOMETRICALLY
11 HUSKIES OF THE BIG EAST
12 HAND (OUT)
14 ___ CURTIS, ONETIME COSMETICS GIANT
20 LION CONSTELLATION
21 TONGUE-CLUCKING SOUNDS
24 PART OF A FEDORA
25 MAKE OVER, AS A KITCHEN
27 RATER OF MPG
28 GRETEL, TO HANSEL
31 SMOOTHED, AS TIMBER
33 FOOTBALL YARDAGE
34 SHRUG-OF-THE-SHOULDERS COMMENT
35 MCKELLEN AND FLEMING
36 POPEYE'S ___'PEA
38 RELUCTANT RISERS
42
44
47 APARTMENT DWELLER
48 "BYE BYE MISS AMERICAN ___"
50 FRAGRANT WOOD
51 ROCKY PROJECTION
53 COME IN SECOND
54 STARLET'S GOAL
55 HAVING FOUR PARTS: PREFIX
56 TRUDGE THROUGH SLUDGE
59 NEW ZEALAND BIRD, ONCE
61 SERPENT'S WARNING

Answers on page 158.

WOMEN IN HISTORY

THIS TEACHER STAYED WITH HELEN KELLER FROM 1887 UNTIL HER OWN DEATH IN 1936	WHO IS ____?
IN THIS WOMAN'S CENTENNIAL YEAR, THE U.S. PASSED THE 19th AMENDMENT THAT ACHIEVED HER GOAL	WHO IS ____?
SHE WAS THE ONLY SURVIVING CHILD OF HENRY VIII'S FIRST WIFE	WHO IS ____?
IN THE LATE 1940s, SHE FOUNDED A FEMALE BRANCH OF HER HUSBAND'S POLITICAL PARTY IN ARGENTINA	WHO IS ____?
TOSCANINI ONCE PRAISED THIS CONTRALTO, SAYING SHE HAD A VOICE THAT COMES "ONCE IN A HUNDRED YEARS"	WHO IS ____?

ANNE FRANK
BETTY FRIEDAN
BOUDICCA
CLARA BARTON
CLEOPATRA
COCO CHANEL
ELIZABETH I
FRIDA KAHLO
HELEN KELLER
INDIRA GANDHI
JANE AUSTEN
JOAN OF ARC
JUDITH BUTLER
MIRABAI
MOTHER TERESA

ROSA PARKS
SACAGAWEA
SAPPHO
SOJOURNER TRUTH

R	I	R	S	T	L	T	C	L	E	O	P	A	T	R	A	A
E	H	E	I	N	D	I	R	A	G	A	N	D	H	I	Z	C
L	T	L	E	I	C	L	A	R	A	B	A	R	T	O	N	C
L	E	T	V	A	S	E	R	E	T	R	E	H	T	O	M	I
E	B	U	A	B	Y	J	R	O	S	A	P	A	R	K	S	D
K	A	B	P	A	N	N	E	S	U	L	L	I	V	A	N	U
N	Z	H	E	R	O	D	U	T	Y	R	A	M	U	W	Y	O
E	I	T	R	I	G	W	C	R	A	F	O	N	A	O	J	B
L	L	I	O	M	O	F	R	I	D	A	K	A	H	L	O	Y
E	E	D	N	O	S	R	E	D	N	A	N	A	I	R	A	M
H	T	U	R	T	R	E	N	R	U	O	J	O	S	Q	L	Y
T	L	J	G	S	U	S	A	N	B	A	N	T	H	O	N	Y
B	E	T	T	Y	F	R	I	E	D	A	N	C	E	K	R	M
O	H	P	P	A	S	S	A	C	A	G	A	W	E	A	J	I
A	N	N	E	F	R	A	N	K	B	S	B	B	L	E	I	K
N	E	T	S	U	A	E	N	A	J	K	D	E	F	L	S	S
C	O	C	O	C	H	A	N	E	L	D	O	J	K	M	I	C

Answers on page 158.

WORD ORIGINS

WHETHER IT'S A PROBLEM IN THE EYE OR A WATERFALL, IT'S FROM THE GREEK FOR "TO DASH DOWN"	WHAT IS ____?
THIS WORD FOR A KIND OF LAND MASS COMES FROM A WORD MEANING "TO CONTAIN"	WHAT IS ____?
THIS TERM FOR A LEADING CHARACTER OF A LITERARY WORK COMES FROM THE GREEK FOR "FIRST COMBATANT"	WHAT IS ____?
FROM THE ITALIAN FOR "BENCH", IT'S A SUMPTUOUS FEAST GIVEN IN SOMEONE'S HONOR	WHAT IS ____?
THIS LARGE, TRIANGULAR SAIL USED ON SOME RACING YACHTS IS SAID TO DERIVE ITS NAME FROM A YACHT CALLED THE SPHINX	WHAT IS ____?

ABACUS	**BARITONE**	**EQUESTRIAN**
ABRASION	**BIBLIOMANIA**	**FELINE**
ACCIPITER	**BICYCLE**	**FISSION**
ACNE	**CANINE**	**GAMMA**
BALLISTIC	**CODA**	**GENESIS**

HALOGEN	**OBELISK**	**URGENCY**
HERESY	**RADIANCE**	**VACILLATE**
INEFFABLE	**RETROGRADE**	**VETO**

Y T E U Q N A B A B R A S I O N S
B I B L I O M A N I A J S L E M N
E D A R G O R T E R B K N T N J I
T E L B A F F E N I P Z S G I N G
E N I L E F M P T N E N I T N O C
B I C Y C L E W R W X X E L A Y L
S P I N N A K E R E T I P I C C A
D E Q U E S T R I A N E X N O L X
B A L L I S T I C Y C D E D W E E
E A P V G Z T S I N O G A T O R P
S U C A B A E A A W R X R L L O V
F I S S I O N I M U Y S E R E H A
M P X K L C D L N M O B E L I S K
C A T A R A C T O B A R I T O N E
I C A K R K V T Q Q N G V A C N E
N H A L O G E N G E N E S I S X M
V R O I H V A C I L L A T E B L D

Answers on page 159.

U.S. CITIES

IT'S THE SOUTHERNMOST STATE CAPITAL	WHAT IS ____?
ITS NICKNAMES INCLUDE "THE ATHENS OF AMERICA" & "THE CRADLE OF LIBERTY"	WHAT IS ____?
BENJAMIN FRANKLIN PARKWAY & THE FRANKLIN INSTITUTE SCIENCE MUSEUM ARE IN THIS CITY	WHAT IS ____?
LOCATED IN THIS CITY'S GARDEN DISTRICT, COMMANDER'S PALACE FEATURES A JAZZ BRUNCH ON WEEKENDS	WHAT IS ____?
W.C. HANDY WROTE SOME OF HIS BLUES ON BEALE STREET IN THIS CITY	WHAT IS ____?

ACROSS

1 BOOK OF MAPS
6 AUTHOR ___ STANLEY GARDNER
10 MADLIKOVA OF TENNIS
14 TICKED AND THEN SOME
15 GET TOGETHER WITH
16 DEDICATED POEMS
17
19 ARROW NOTCH
20 VOLUNTEER ST.
21 THE EMERALD ISLE, TO POETS
22 SWEETLY, IN MUSIC
23 COLOR NAMED FOR A BIRD
26 LEAR'S TREACHEROUS DAUGHTER
29 "THE JUNGLE BOOK" STAR
30 U.S. 1, E.G.
31 WHAT RINGS LACK
33 PATRON OF SURGEONS
37 PERCHED ON OR TOY?

39 "NOT MY SPELLING ERROR" NOTATION
41 SPORT ___ (OFF-ROAD VEHICLES)
42
45 SMALL VALLEY
48 LIKELY (TO)
49 OLD MARRIAGE VOW WORD
51
53
57 POE'S "NEVERMORE" SPEAKER
58 UPHOLSTERED COUCH
59 BRING DOWN THE QUARTERBACK
63 LEVINE OF "THE VOICE"
64 AMBITION
66 SAY NO TO
67 WORD WITH "GROUP" OR "PRESSURE"
68 BLAKLEY OF "NASHVILLE"
69 ITALIAN PROVINCE NOTED FOR WINE
70 "IN ___" (BASICALLY)
71 LIKE OIL DIRECTLY FROM A WELL

DOWN

1 GERSHWIN'S "IT ___ NECESSARILY SO"
2 SQUIRREL'S REFUGE
3 HOMEOWNER'S GRASSY AREA
4 "STAT!"
5 SUNDAY DELIVERY, FOR SHORT
6 GREEN GEMSTONES
7 SHOW, AS AN OLD SITCOM
8 BRUCE AND KRAVITZ
9 UFO RIDERS
10
11 "BE ___": "HELP ME OUT"
12 CANDY WAFER BRAND
13 SLIGHTLY OFF-CENTER
18 SOVIET ENTOMBED IN RED SQUARE
22 ITEM IN THE RED
24 "JUST THE WAY YOU ___" (BRUNO MARS HIT)
25 ___ IN "YANKEE"
26 TAKE RUDELY
27 SGT. SNORKEL'S DOG
28 AVANT-GARDE SORTS
32 "___ THE SCIENCE KID" (PBS SERIES)
34 SUNDANCE FILM FESTIVAL STATE
35 DE GAULLE TRADEMARK
36 INEXACT FIGURES, BRIEFLY
38 ANCIENT DYNASTY FOUNDER
40 PLACE FOR OUTDOOR STORYTELLING
43 SCOTTISH RESORT TOWN
44 NEIGHBOR OF HOMER AND MARGE
46 "THE MERRY WIDOW" COMPOSER FRANZ
47 BRITISH RECORD LABEL UNTIL 2012
50 AGREEABLE RESPONSES
52 MINISTER
53 "THE DEVIL WEARS ___"
54 UNDERWORLD OF GREEK MYTH
55 "___ TO BE ALONE" (WORDS ATTRIBUTED TO GRETA GARBO)
56 BOUNDS ALONG EASILY
60 HOKKAIDO NATIVE
61 CAMPUS LASS
62 LEG HINGE
64 BARBARY PRIMATE
65 RAINBOW CURVE

Answers on page 159.

WEIGHTS & MEASURES

THE NAME OF THIS NAUTICAL MEASURE OF DEPTH CAN ALSO MEAN "COMPREHEND"

WHAT IS ____?

FOR PETROLEUM, 42 U.S. GALLONS IS ONE OF THESE UNITS

WHAT IS ____?

ONE UNIT OF THIS DISTANCE USED IN HORSE RACING IS EXACTLY 660 FEET

WHAT IS ____?

ONE QUIRE IS 25 SHEETS OF PAPER, OR 1/20th OF AN ORDINARY ONE OF THESE

WHAT IS ____?

THIS U.K. MEASURE OF 14 U.S. POUNDS HAS ALSO BEEN USED FOR 16 POUNDS OF CHEESE

WHAT IS ____?

ACROSS

1
6 UTTER UNCLEARLY
10
14 ___ NOIR (RED WINE)
15 MAKE LESS DIFFICULT
16 NO LONGER DECEIVED BY
17 TYPE OF COFFEE, LINEN OR SETTER
18 YEOMAN'S YESES
19 AT THE HIGHEST POINT OF
20 FARTHEST DOWN
22 ENJOY A FINE RESTAURANT
23 UNDERWATER HAZARD
24 ADDED SEASONINGS TO
26 THE VAIN PUT THEM ON
30 THE FACTS, FOR SHORT
32 CONSIDERS CAREFULLY, AS ADVICE
33 PASTURE SOUND
35 GUEST'S CRASH PAD

37
39 GETS CRACKING
44 COW-HORNED GODDESS
46 EXTREME FEAR
47 NOVEL FEATURES
51 FIRST CAR TO OFFER SEAT BELTS
53 FABLED HIMALAYAN CREATURE
54
56 LAY ___ THICK (FLATTER)
58 NEPAL'S CONTINENT
59 PUT IN THE SPOTLIGHT
65 ONE SIXTY-BILLIONTH OF A MIN.
66 ROBIN'S MARIAN, FOR ONE
67 BIRTHPLACE OF COLUMBUS
68 DROP SHOT, IN TENNIS
69 FORMER HAWKS ARENA
70 CERBERUS GUARDS ITS ENTRANCE
71 WEST SIDE STORY GANG
72 STARCH FROM A PALM
73 CLANDESTINE MEET-UP

DOWN

1 DAMAGE CONTROL TACTIC
2 LOSE PEP
3 "STEP ___!" ("HURRY UP!")
4 SMALL SNACK
5 UPPER REGIONS OF SPACE, FIGURATIVELY
6 SALTS
7 WORKFORCE REDUCTIONS
8 PUTS INTO SERVICE
9 TIMES TO RELAX
10 BAND FOLLOWER
11 TEMPT
12 MADE UP FOR
13 BERMUDA BIKES
21 OCCUPIES THE THRONE
25 PART OF A MOON CYCLE
26 WISE-CRACKING SITCOM ALIEN
27 PROMISSORY NOTE
28 PRESIDENT BEFORE GHWB
29 THE "S" IN "RSVP"
31 SOUND HEARD DURING FIREWORKS
34 REALLY BAD MUSIC, TO THE LISTENER
36
38 KIND OF RUMMY
40 HEAR, AS A CASE
41 BEFORE, IN SONNETS
42 MICHAEL JACKSON'S "YOU ARE ___ ALONE"
43 ___ LANKA (ASIAN ISLAND NATION)
45 ON THE MOVE ON THE BRINY
47 POPULAR SANDWICH FOR KIDS, FOR SHORT
48 TV COLLIE
49 POSITION PROPERLY
50 SIGNS OF WILDLIFE
52 RECORDING ROOM
55 PROM NIGHT RENTALS
57 DRACULA'S SHIFT
60 TIBETAN PRIEST
61 WARM, IN A GUESSING GAME
62 GARCIA OF "OCEAN'S ELEVEN"
63 TOT'S "LITTLE PIGGIES"
64 JET STREAM DIRECTION

Answers on page 160.

WORLD RELIGIONS

ONCE A YEAR MEMBERS OF THIS RELIGION PAY A TAX CALLED ZAKAT, ARABIC FOR "PURIFICATION"	WHAT IS ____?
2 OF THE ANCIENT HOLY BOOKS OF THIS JAPANESE RELIGION ARE THE KOJIKI & THE NIHONGI	WHAT IS ____?
MORE THAN 80% OF INDIA'S PEOPLE PRACTICE THIS RELIGION	WHAT IS ____?
THIS RELIGIOUS MOVEMENT WAS FOUNDED IN JAMAICA AROUND 1930	WHAT IS ____?
THE FOUNDER OF THIS PERSIAN-BASED RELIGION DIED IN 1892 IN A PRISON COLONY	WHAT IS ____?

BAPTIST
BUDDHISM
CATHOLICISM
DEISM
DRUIDISM
EVANGELICAL
FOLK
GNOSTICISM
HUMANISM
JAINISM
JUDAISM
PAGANISM
SANTERIA
SCIENTOLOGY
SIKHISM

TAOISM
WICCA

W	P	Z	B	R	V	Z	M	S	I	A	D	U	J	S	E	K
X	J	M	M	S	G	G	A	F	Q	N	E	M	A	H	V	Z
D	T	S	S	Q	I	C	V	Z	K	F	A	A	I	I	A	W
R	D	A	C	I	C	K	F	C	I	N	G	L	N	N	N	G
U	N	N	M	I	N	P	H	E	O	A	K	S	I	T	G	Z
I	T	T	W	S	E	A	R	I	A	K	H	I	S	O	E	H
D	E	E	B	S	I	N	I	H	S	B	A	A	M	J	L	U
I	U	R	M	U	G	C	T	R	I	M	K	X	B	T	I	M
S	P	I	N	S	D	N	I	O	A	P	K	L	O	F	C	A
M	A	A	T	K	I	D	O	L	L	F	X	D	R	Z	A	N
C	G	U	N	S	D	U	H	S	O	O	A	W	H	T	L	I
V	A	E	D	X	I	M	D	I	T	H	G	T	G	H	Q	S
I	N	C	I	E	S	T	G	N	S	I	T	Y	S	S	V	M
T	I	O	O	I	I	G	P	O	I	M	C	A	R	A	P	B
A	S	F	O	A	V	S	G	A	S	H	H	I	C	U	R	T
R	M	A	V	Y	S	F	M	B	B	Z	X	M	S	S	L	U
T	T	H	N	X	X	A	J	L	K	G	A	H	D	M	Z	H

Answers on page 160.

ANSWER KEY

PAINTERS (PAGE 4)

ANSWER 1:
WHO IS PABLO PICASSO? (43 ACROSS)
ANSWER 2:
WHO IS LEONARDO DA VINCI? (36 ACROSS)
ANSWER 3:
WHO IS JACKSON POLLOCK? (49 ACROSS)
ANSWER 4:
WHAT IS "AMERICAN GOTHIC"? (20 ACROSS)
ANSWER 5:
WHO IS MARAT? (47 DOWN)

STATE CAPITALS (PAGE 6)

ANSWER 1:
WHAT IS AUGUSTA?
ANSWER 2:
WHAT IS MONTPELIER?
ANSWER 3:
WHAT IS TOPEKA?
ANSWER 4:
WHAT IS BISMARCK?
ANSWER 5:
WHAT IS JUNEAU?

AFRICAN-AMERICAN HISTORY (PAGE 8)

ANSWER 1:
WHAT IS (THE) TRUMPET?
ANSWER 2:
WHAT ARE BUSES?
ANSWER 3:
WHO IS PAUL ROBESON?
ANSWER 4:
WHAT IS HOWARD?
ANSWER 5:
WHAT IS TULSA?

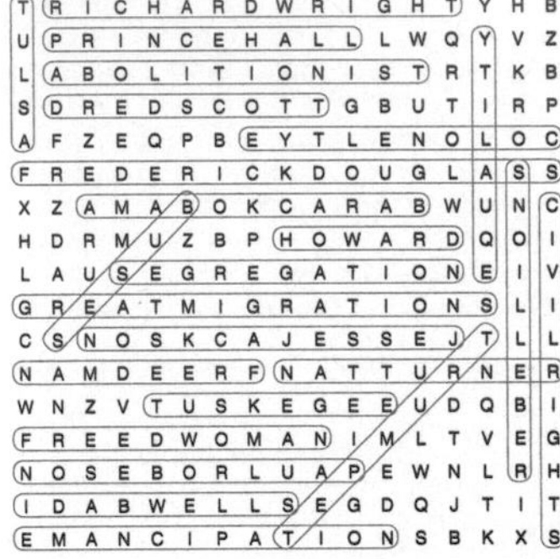

20th CENTURY WARS (PAGE 10)

ANSWER 1:
WHAT IS MADRID? (29 ACROSS)
ANSWER 2:
WHAT IS KUWAIT? (27 ACROSS)
ANSWER 3:
WHAT IS (THE) TANK? (10 ACROSS)
ANSWER 4:
WHAT IS OMAHA? (54 DOWN)
ANSWER 5:
WHAT IS MAU-MAU? (31 DOWN)

ANSWER KEY

AUTHORS (PAGE 12)

ANSWER 1:
WHO IS KURT VONNEGUT?
ANSWER 2:
WHO IS TONI MORRISON?
ANSWER 3:
WHO IS DASHIELL HAMMETT?
ANSWER 4:
WHO IS JACK LONDON?
ANSWER 5:
WHAT IS SHAFFER?

ART (PAGE 14)

ANSWER 1:
WHAT ARE BRUSHSTROKES? (27 ACROSS)
ANSWER 2:
WHO IS FRIDA KAHLO? (59 ACROSS)
ANSWER 3:
WHO IS NIKE? (1 ACROSS)
ANSWER 4:
WHAT IS REALISM? (21 ACROSS)
ANSWER 5:
WHAT IS OIL? (40 DOWN)

BODIES OF WATER (PAGE 16)

ANSWER 1:
WHAT IS LAKE SUPERIOR?
ANSWER 2:
WHAT IS (THE) AMAZON RIVER?
ANSWER 3:
WHAT IS (THE) CASPIAN SEA?
ANSWER 4:
WHAT IS RIGA?
ANSWER 5:
WHAT IS LAKE TANGANYIKA?

BUSINESS & INDUSTRY (PAGE 18)

ANSWER 1:
WHAT IS (A) BAILOUT?
ANSWER 2:
WHAT WAS (THE) MODEL T?
ANSWER 3:
WHAT IS (AN) ANGEL?
ANSWER 4:
WHAT ARE EYEBALLS?
ANSWER 5:
WHAT IS STEEL?

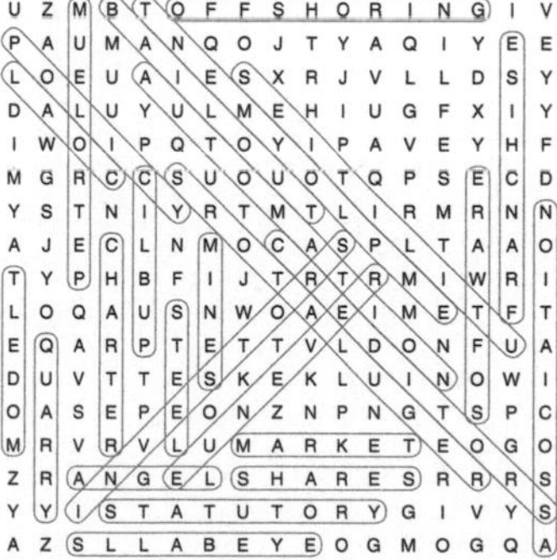

ANSWER KEY

COLONIAL AMERICA (PAGE 20)

ANSWER 1:
WHAT IS VIRGINIA? (1 ACROSS)
ANSWER 2:
WHAT IS SPAIN? (50 ACROSS)
ANSWER 3:
WHAT IS NEW JERSEY? (32 DOWN)
ANSWER 4:
WHAT IS DELAWARE? (67 ACROSS)
ANSWER 5:
WHAT IS MANHATTAN? (11 DOWN)

■	V	I	R	G	I	N	I	A	■	I	N	M	A	N
A	I	R	C	A	N	A	D	A	■	O	R	A	L	E
S	T	R	A	T	A	G	E	M	■	T	O	N	T	O
T	A	E	■	E	R	A	S	■	L	A	T	H	E	■
O	L	G	A	■	U	N	T	I	E	■	C	A	R	D
■	■	■	N	A	T	O	■	D	I	S	■	T	E	A
■	N	I	N	E	■	■	A	L	A	E	■	T	G	I
Z	E	N	E	R	■	A	C	E	■	C	H	A	O	S
A	W	K	■	I	A	M	S	■	■	T	O	N	S	■
P	J	S	■	E	S	A	■	L	A	S	H	■	■	■
S	E	T	H	■	S	P	A	I	N	■	O	A	T	H
■	R	A	Y	O	N	■	N	O	G	S	■	S	A	I
A	S	I	N	K	■	M	O	N	O	L	I	T	H	S
L	E	N	D	L	■	I	T	E	R	A	T	I	O	N
B	Y	S	E	A	■	D	E	L	A	W	A	R	E	■

EAST OF THE MISSISSIPPI (PAGE 22)

ANSWER 1:
WHAT IS NASHVILLE?
ANSWER 2:
WHAT IS SELMA?
ANSWER 3:
WHAT IS KEY WEST?
ANSWER 4:
WHAT IS LOUISVILLE?
ANSWER 5:
WHAT IS SARATOGA SPRINGS?

EXPLORERS (PAGE 24)

ANSWER 1:
WHAT IS ROANOKE?
ANSWER 2:
WHO IS JAMES COOK?
ANSWER 3:
WHO IS VASCO DA GAMA?
ANSWER 4:
WHO IS VITUS BERING?
ANSWER 5:
WHO IS (SIR) FRANCIS DRAKE?

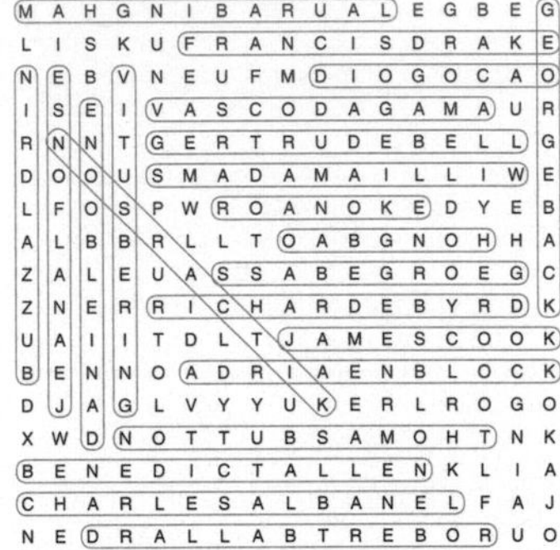

DISCOVERIES (PAGE 26)

ANSWER 1:
WHAT IS (THE) GOBI? (34 ACROSS)
ANSWER 2:
WHAT IS SUGAR? (1 DOWN)
ANSWER 3:
WHAT ARE CELLS? (57 DOWN)
ANSWER 4:
WHAT IS HYDROGEN? (64 ACROSS)
ANSWER 5:
WHAT IS ELECTRICITY? (40 ACROSS)

S	A	S	S	E	S	■	S	E	A	S	C	A	P	E
U	N	T	A	P	E	■	I	D	I	T	A	R	O	D
G	A	M	B	I	T	■	M	A	D	E	S	U	R	E
A	D	A	■	C	A	W	■	M	A	L	I	■	■	■
R	E	L	E	N	T	E	D	■	■	E	N	D	E	D
■	M	O	T	O	■	B	E	E	P	■	G	O	B	I
■	■	■	A	V	A	■	A	L	I	T	■	R	B	I
■	■	E	L	E	C	T	R	I	C	I	T	Y	■	■
E	T	A	■	L	E	I	S	■	T	E	A	■	■	■
M	A	R	S	■	S	A	I	D	■	S	L	O	G	■
S	E	P	I	A	■	■	R	I	C	O	C	H	E	T
■	■	■	E	C	O	L	■	G	E	N	■	S	T	A
H	Y	D	R	O	G	E	N	■	L	E	P	T	O	N
A	M	A	R	I	L	L	O	■	L	O	G	O	U	T
B	A	T	A	N	E	Y	E	■	S	N	A	P	T	O

ANSWER KEY

FIRST LADIES (PAGE 28)

ANSWER 1:
WHO IS HILLARY RODHAM?
ANSWER 2:
WHO IS PAT NIXON?
ANSWER 3:
WHO IS BARBARA BUSH?
ANSWER 4:
WHO IS MAMIE EISENHOWER?
ANSWER 5:
WHO IS DOLLEY MADISON?

ISLANDS (PAGE 32)

ANSWER 1:
WHAT IS TAHITI?
ANSWER 2:
WHAT IS SRI LANKA?
ANSWER 3:
WHAT ARE (THE) AZORES?
ANSWER 4:
WHAT IS HONSHU?
ANSWER 5:
WHAT IS LUZON?

ENDS IN "ISM" (PAGE 30)

ANSWER 1:
WHAT IS EXISTENTIALISM? (47 ACROSS)
ANSWER 2:
WHAT IS SOLECISM? (41 DOWN)
ANSWER 3:
WHAT IS (AN) ANACHRONISM? (17 ACROSS)
ANSWER 4:
WHAT IS SIKHISM? (53 ACROSS)
ANSWER 5:
WHAT IS PURITANISM? (28 ACROSS)

ENDS IN "TT" (PAGE 34)

ANSWER 1:
WHAT IS (A) PUTT? (60 DOWN)
ANSWER 2:
WHAT IS (A) KILOWATT? (38 DOWN)
ANSWER 3:
WHAT IS BABBITT? (51 ACROSS)
ANSWER 4:
WHAT IS (A) LETT? (1 DOWN)
ANSWER 5:
WHAT IS NARRAGANSETT? (23 ACROSS)

ANSWER KEY

LITERATURE (PAGE 36)

ANSWER 1:
WHAT IS ENGLISH?
ANSWER 2:
WHAT IS "DUBLINERS"?
ANSWER 3:
WHO WAS OSCAR WILDE?
ANSWER 4:
WHAT IS PAMPLONA?
ANSWER 5:
WHO IS HERMAN MELVILLE?

NEW YORK CITY (PAGE 38)

ANSWER 1:
WHAT IS (A) TUNNEL?
ANSWER 2:
WHAT IS BROADWAY?
ANSWER 3:
WHAT IS TRIBECA?
ANSWER 4:
WHAT IS (THE) JUILLIARD (SCHOOL)?
ANSWER 5:
WHAT IS LONG ISLAND?

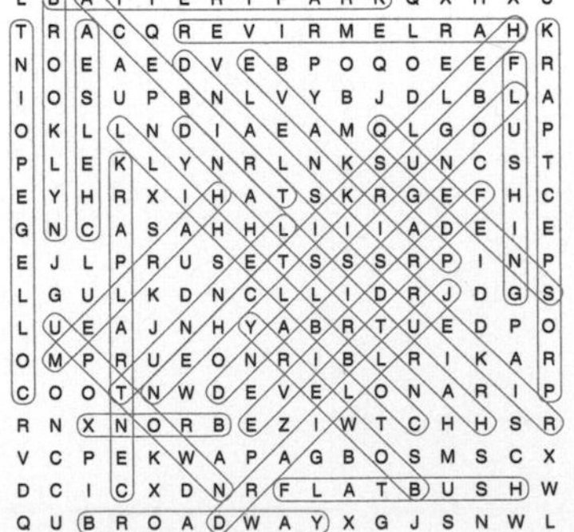

MUSIC (PAGE 40)

ANSWER 1:
WHO IS CARLY SIMON? (17 ACROSS)
ANSWER 2:
WHO IS PHARRELL? (25 ACROSS)
ANSWER 3:
WHO IS JANIS JOPLIN? (48 ACROSS)
ANSWER 4:
WHAT IS "TOMMY"? (64 ACROSS)
ANSWER 5:
WHO IS KENDRICK LAMAR? (33 ACROSS)

Z	E	N	D	A		A	R	E	S		I	N	T	S
A	L	O	E	S		S	A	G	A		N	E	U	N
C	A	R	L	Y	S	I	M	O	N		T	A	P	A
	M	O	L	E	S				T	A	U	T	E	R
A	T	A	R	U	N		P	H	A	R	R	E	L	L
R	O	R	E	M		A	A	U		A	N	N	O	Y
N	C	A	A		O	S	T	L	E	R				
	K	E	N	D	R	I	C	K	L	A	M	A	R	
				B	L	A	H		S	T	E	N	O	S
F	L	O	R	A		G	U	S			N	A	T	O
J	A	N	I	S	J	O	P	L	I	N		G	O	B
O	N	S	P	E	C			I	N	O	U	R		
R	A	T	E		R	E	C	E	N	T	P	A	S	T
D	I	A	N		E	N	D	S		T	O	M	M	Y
S	S	R	S		W	E	S	T		E	N	S	U	E

ANSWER KEY

POETS AND POETRY (PAGE 42)

ANSWER 1:
WHAT IS "THE BELLS"?
ANSWER 2:
WHAT IS (THE) ROMANTIC?
ANSWER 3:
WHO IS EMILY DICKINSON?
ANSWER 4:
WHO IS MAYA ANGELOU?
ANSWER 5:
WHO IS LAURA?

MYTHOLOGY (PAGE 44)

ANSWER 1:
WHAT IS RICE? (35 ACROSS)
ANSWER 2:
WHAT IS (A) SPIDER? (22 ACROSS)
ANSWER 3:
WHAT IS (THE) GOLEM? (27 DOWN)
ANSWER 4:
WHAT IS ASGARD? (54 ACROSS)
ANSWER 5:
WHAT IS SCYLLA? (6 DOWN)

POTENT POTABLES (PAGE 46)

ANSWER 1:
WHAT IS CHAMPAGNE?
ANSWER 2:
WHAT IS KAHLUA?
ANSWER 3:
WHAT IS (A) PINA COLADA?
ANSWER 4:
WHAT IS MEAD?
ANSWER 5:
WHAT IS GIN?

ANSWER KEY

POTPOURRI (PAGE 48)

ANSWER 1:
WHO IS MATHEW BRADY?
ANSWER 2:
WHO IS FRANK OZ?
ANSWER 3:
WHAT IS JAI ALAI?
ANSWER 4:
WHAT IS "FAMILY MATTERS"?
ANSWER 5:
WHAT ARE MUSSELS?

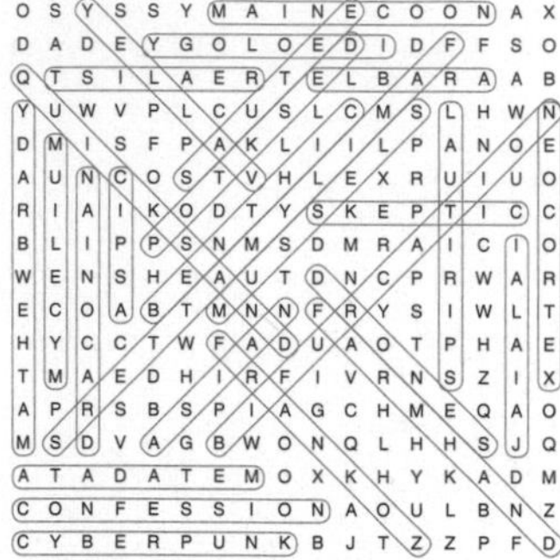

RIVERS (PAGE 50)

ANSWER 1:
WHAT IS (THE) NILE? (61 ACROSS)
ANSWER 2:
WHAT IS (THE) THAMES? (9 DOWN)
ANSWER 3:
WHAT IS (THE) PO? (31 ACROSS)
ANSWER 4:
WHAT IS (THE) MISSOURI? (5 DOWN)
ANSWER 5:
WHAT IS (THE) INDUS? (12 DOWN)

U.S. PRESIDENTS (PAGE 52)

ANSWER 1:
WHO IS TEDDY ROOSEVELT?
ANSWER 2:
WHO IS RICHARD NIXON?
ANSWER 3:
WHAT IS JEFFERSON?
ANSWER 4:
WHAT IS MEXICO?
ANSWER 5:
WHO IS JAMES MADISON?

D E T C E L E C X I G J X W H I G
I N A U G U R A T I O N S Z Z M Q
N V Q Y U G E R A L D F O R D P N
O N O X I N D R A H C I R R F E V
S P F I N O I N U L A N O I T A N
R T E D D Y R O O S E V E L T C H
E G D S Y A D N O I T C E L E H J
F R E V O O H T R E B R E H N E I
F B R I W J F R K J Y N Q F G D M
E P A R D O N D I P L O M A C Y M
J M L R O N A L D R E A G A N Y Y
U L I U H O C I X E M Y V O Z X C
U M S S U C C E S S I O N T M A A
Z I T V I C E P R E S I D E N T R
F O R E I G N P O L I C Y V X N T
C O M M A N D E R I N C H I E F E
N O S I D A M S E M A J P P V J R

ANSWER KEY

SCIENCE (PAGE 54)

ANSWER 1:
WHAT IS SEDIMENTARY? (44 ACROSS)
ANSWER 2:
WHAT ARE GYMNOSPERMS? (26 ACROSS)
ANSWER 3:
WHAT IS WATER? (49 ACROSS)
ANSWER 4:
WHAT IS (A) LOBOTOMY? (52 ACROSS)
ANSWER 5:
WHAT IS IONIZATION? (18 ACROSS)

U.S. HISTORY (PAGE 56)

ANSWER 1:
WHO IS SACAJAWEA?
ANSWER 2:
WHAT IS OHIO?
ANSWER 3:
WHAT ARE TEARS?
ANSWER 4:
WHAT IS (THE) DUST BOWL?
ANSWER 5:
WHAT IS TEAPOT DOME?

WEST OF THE MISSISSIPPI (PAGE 58)

ANSWER 1:
WHAT IS WYOMING?
ANSWER 2:
WHAT IS LAS CRUCES?
ANSWER 3:
WHAT IS EUGENE?
ANSWER 4:
WHAT IS GARLIC?
ANSWER 5:
WHAT IS (THE) CONTINENTAL?

ANSWER KEY

SHAKESPEARE (PAGE 60)

ANSWER 1:
WHO IS OTHELLO? (53 ACROSS)
ANSWER 2:
WHO IS FALSTAFF? (10 DOWN)
ANSWER 3:
WHAT IS "THE TEMPEST"? (16 ACROSS)
ANSWER 4:
WHO IS KING LEAR? (36 DOWN)
ANSWER 5:
WHAT IS ELSINORE? (35 DOWN)

A	R	G	O	N		R	O	M	E			F	D	R
T	A	R	S	I		E	L	I	A		S	A	N	E
T	H	E	T	E	M	P	E	S	T		P	L	A	T
I	R	E		C	E	E		C	A	R	E	S	T	O
L	A	N	T	E	R	N			B	E	T	T	E	R
A	H	S	O		I	T	S	E	L	F		A	S	T
			M	A	T		C	L	E	O		F	T	S
	E	K	E	D		S	E	A		R	E	F	S	
A	L	I		E	C	O	N		A	M	A			
S	S	N		X	A	N	A	D	U		S	E	C	T
S	I	G	N	E	T			O	T	H	E	L	L	O
U	N	L	A	C	E	S		M	O	E		L	E	T
M	O	E	T		R	E	D	A	S	A	B	E	E	T
E	R	A	S		E	T	U	I		T	E	R	S	E
S	E	R			R	I	E	N		S	L	Y	E	R

WITTY QUOTES (PAGE 62)

ANSWER 1:
WHO WAS H. L. MENCKEN?
ANSWER 2:
WHO WAS SAMUEL JOHNSON?
ANSWER 3:
WHO WAS DOROTHY PARKER?
ANSWER 4:
WHO IS TOM WOLFE?
ANSWER 5:
WHO IS YOGI BERRA?

WEIRD NATURE (PAGE 64)

ANSWER 1:
WHAT ARE CAMELS? (31 ACROSS)
ANSWER 2:
WHAT IS ANTARCTICA? (17 ACROSS)
ANSWER 3:
WHAT IS POLLEN? (59 ACROSS)
ANSWER 4:
WHAT ARE FEATHERS? (53 ACROSS)
ANSWER 5:
WHAT ARE (THE) LEGS? (35 DOWN)

ANSWER KEY

WOMEN AUTHORS (PAGE 66)

ANSWER 1:
WHO IS AMY TAN?
ANSWER 2:
WHAT IS RIPLEY?
ANSWER 3:
WHO IS ANNE RICE?
ANSWER 4:
WHAT IS "THE HOURS"?
ANSWER 5:
WHO IS ZADIE SMITH?

WORLD CAPITALS (PAGE 68)

ANSWER 1:
WHAT IS OSLO?
ANSWER 2:
WHAT IS KATHMANDU?
ANSWER 3:
WHAT IS RABAT?
ANSWER 4:
WHAT IS WARSAW?
ANSWER 5:
WHAT IS KINSHASA?

WORLD HISTORY (PAGE 70)

ANSWER 1:
WHO IS KUBLAI KHAN? (60 ACROSS)
ANSWER 2:
WHAT IS TIMBUKTU? (39 DOWN)
ANSWER 3:
WHAT IS SHOGUN? (20 ACROSS)
ANSWER 4:
WHAT IS THE CONQUEROR? (27 ACROSS)
ANSWER 5:
WHAT IS PUNIC? (51 DOWN)

H	A	R	M	■	P	E	P	U	P	■	L	A	D	S
A	M	O	K	■	R	O	U	S	H	■	A	R	E	A
W	A	L	T	D	I	S	N	E	Y	■	O	P	E	D
S	H	O	G	U	N	■	Y	E	S	I	T	S	M	E
E	L	S	■	C	C	S	■	■	I	M	S	■	■	■
■	■	■	T	H	E	C	O	N	Q	U	E	R	O	R
S	A	T	A	Y	■	L	A	I	U	S	■	E	R	O
U	S	E	D	■	T	E	R	S	E	■	A	F	T	S
B	E	E	■	S	I	R	E	E	■	S	W	I	S	S
J	A	M	E	S	M	A	D	I	S	O	N	■	■	■
■	■	■	S	T	B	■	■	S	T	D	■	A	S	P
T	R	E	A	S	U	R	E	■	M	O	O	S	H	U
H	I	L	L	■	K	U	B	L	A	I	K	H	A	N
E	L	S	E	■	T	I	B	E	R	■	L	O	K	I
E	L	A	N	■	U	N	S	A	Y	■	A	W	A	C

ANSWER KEY

ANAGRAMMED WORLD LEADERS (PAGE 72)

ANSWER 1:
WHO IS VLADIMIR PUTIN?
ANSWER 2:
WHO IS THERESA MAY?
ANSWER 3:
WHO IS ANGELA MERKEL?
ANSWER 4:
WHO IS JUSTIN TRUDEAU?
ANSWER 5:
WHO IS RAUL CASTRO?

FEMALE INVENTORS (PAGE 74)

ANSWER 1:
WHAT IS (A) WINDSHIELD WIPER?
ANSWER 2:
WHAT IS SCOTCHGARD?
ANSWER 3:
WHAT IS KEVLAR?
ANSWER 4:
WHAT ARE SIGNAL FLARES?
ANSWER 5:
WHAT IS (THE) SNUGLI?

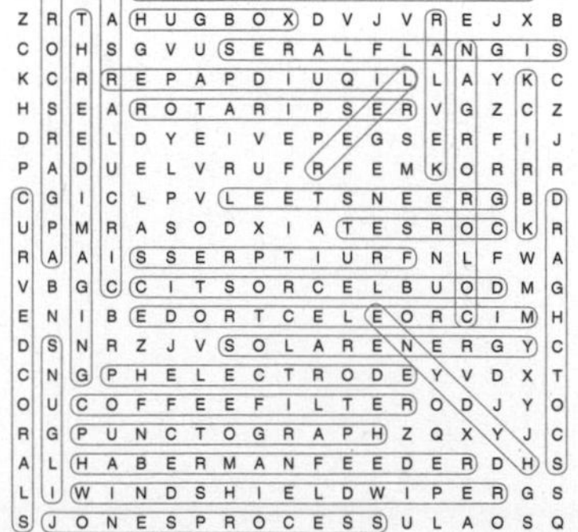

10-LETTER WORDS (PAGE 76)

ANSWER 1:
WHAT IS BLACKSMITH? (29 DOWN)
ANSWER 2:
WHAT IS ABOMINABLE? (13 ACROSS)
ANSWER 3:
WHAT IS MASQUERADE? (10 DOWN)
ANSWER 4:
WHAT IS CYBERSPACE? (41 ACROSS)
ANSWER 5:
WHAT IS WOODPECKER? (62 ACROSS)

P	A	N	E	■	A	L	A	I	■	■	H	M	O	S
A	B	O	M	I	N	A	B	L	E	■	M	A	N	Y
D	E	L	E	C	T	A	B	L	E	■	S	S	T	S
■	D	A	R	E	I	■	R	T	E	S	■	Q	A	T
■	■	■	I	M	S	O	■	R	E	A	D	U	P	■
T	A	B	L	E	■	A	N	Y	■	R	U	E	■	■
O	R	L	■	N	A	T	O	■	R	A	M	R	O	D
U	N	A	S	■	C	Y	B	E	R	S	P	A	C	E
R	O	C	K	N	E	■	L	D	S	■	S	D	A	K
■	■	K	I	A	■	B	Y	O	■	U	S	E	S	A
■	A	S	P	I	R	E	■	M	Y	S	T	■	■	■
B	U	M	■	R	O	M	P	■	A	H	O	O	T	■
A	D	I	N	■	W	O	O	D	P	E	C	K	E	R
S	I	T	E	■	E	A	R	M	A	R	K	I	N	G
S	O	H	O	■	■	N	E	A	T	■	S	E	N	T

ANSWER KEY

FICTIONAL CHARACTERS (PAGE 78)

ANSWER 1:
WHO IS BETH?
ANSWER 2:
WHO IS STUART LITTLE?
ANSWER 3:
WHO IS UNCLE HENRY?
ANSWER 4:
WHO IS PHILEAS FOGG?
ANSWER 5:
WHO IS BRIDGET JONES?

ANIMAL WORDS (PAGE 80)

ANSWER 1:
WHAT IS STAG? (1 ACROSS)
ANSWER 2:
WHAT IS (A) MONKEY? (48 ACROSS)
ANSWER 3:
WHAT IS (A) BAT? (34 DOWN)
ANSWER 4:
WHAT IS CARP? (57 ACROSS)
ANSWER 5:
WHAT IS (A) VIXEN? (58 ACROSS)

FROM THE LATIN FOR... (PAGE 82)

ANSWER 1:
WHAT IS (A) TRACTOR?
ANSWER 2:
WHAT IS SURROGATE?
ANSWER 3:
WHAT IS REPATRIATION?
ANSWER 4:
WHAT IS (THE) AMBIENCE?
ANSWER 5:
WHAT IS (A) FOUNDRY?

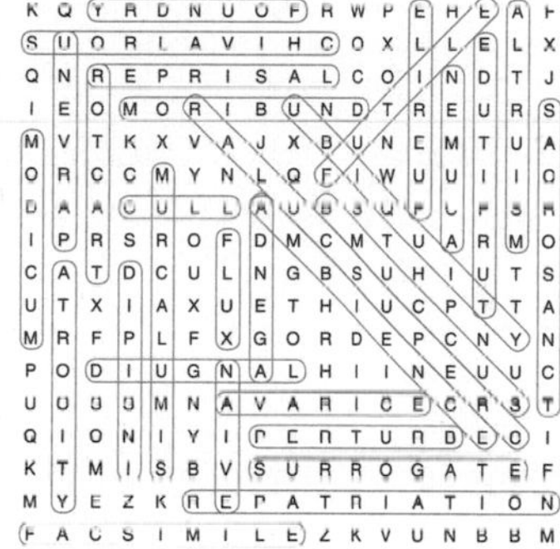

ANSWER KEY

BEST PICTURE OSCAR WINNERS (PAGE 84)

ANSWER 1:
WHAT IS "WEST SIDE STORY"? (34 ACROSS)
ANSWER 2:
WHAT IS "THE ARTIST"? (16 ACROSS)
ANSWER 3:
WHAT IS "BIRDMAN"? (46 ACROSS)
ANSWER 4:
WHAT IS "GLADIATOR"? (54 ACROSS)
ANSWER 5:
WHAT IS "PLATOON"? (24 ACROSS)

R	A	M	P		P	U	N	T			N	A	D	A
E	A	R	L		A	M	O	K		D	O	P	E	Y
T	H	E	A	R	T	I	S	T		A	N	O	L	E
			N	O	O	N	E		A	D	E			
A	B	S	T	A	I	N		P	L	A	T	O	O	N
P	R	E	E	N	S		A	L	I	I		C	N	S
T	E	R	R			A	R	I	A	S		A	E	C
	W	E	S	T	S	I	D	E	S	T	O	R	Y	
S	S	N		H	A	D	E	S			C	I	E	L
I	K	E		I	R	A	N		S	H	A	N	A	S
B	I	R	D	M	A	N		C	L	I	P	A	R	T
			I	B	N		S	H	I	F	T			
C	A	N	A	L		G	L	A	D	I	A	T	O	R
A	D	E	L	E		R	O	S	E		I	R	O	N
D	O	T	S			S	E	E	S		N	A	P	A

HEALTH AND MEDICINE (PAGE 86)

ANSWER 1:
WHAT IS (A) SPINAL TAP?
ANSWER 2:
WHAT IS SECOND DEGREE?
ANSWER 3:
WHAT IS (A) MUSCLE?
ANSWER 4:
WHAT IS (THE) LIVER?
ANSWER 5:
WHO IS LOU GEHRIG?

IN SAN FRANCISCO (PAGE 88)

ANSWER 1:
WHAT ARE CABLE CARS?
ANSWER 2:
WHAT IS WILLIE MAYS?
ANSWER 3:
WHAT IS ASHBURY STREET?
ANSWER 4:
WHAT IS LOMBARD STREET?
ANSWER 5:
WHAT IS PACIFIC?

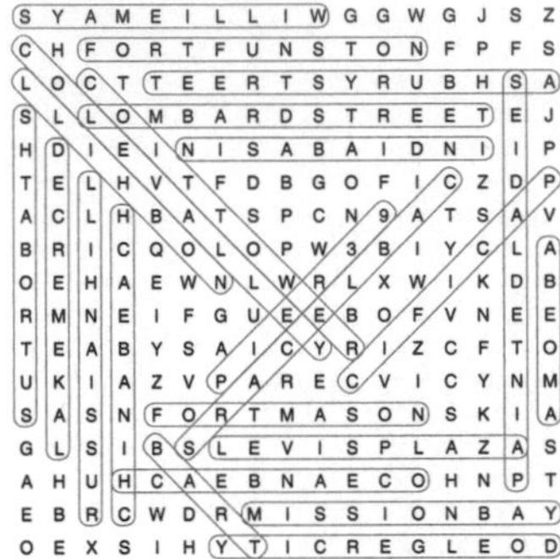

ANSWER KEY

BROADWAY MUSICALS BY SHOWS (PAGE 90)

ANSWER 1:
WHAT IS "GUYS & DOLLS"? (50 ACROSS)
ANSWER 2:
WHAT IS "ANNIE"? (13 DOWN)
ANSWER 3:
WHAT IS "ROCK OF AGES"? (61 ACROSS)
ANSWER 4:
WHAT IS "OKLAHOMA!"? (31 ACROSS)
ANSWER 5:
WHAT IS "THE KING & I"? (21 ACROSS)

L	Y	R	I	C		I	B	I	S		H	A	H	A
L	E	O	N	A		N	O	O	K		O	M	E	N
B	A	N	A	L		T	O	N	I		S	E	I	N
S	R	S		T	H	E	K	I	N	G	A	N	D	I
			P	E	O	R	I	A		U	N	T	I	E
H	I	B	A	C	H	I		N	A	A	N			
O	K	L	A	H	O	M	A		S	M	A	R	T	S
L	E	A	R				G	P	S			O	R	E
D	A	B		S	A	B	R	A		C	U	T	I	E
			M	E	N	E		L	A	M	P	O	O	N
G	U	Y	S	A	N	D	D	O	L	L	S			
L	S	A	T	S		R	E	O	S		C	A	S	E
O	O	L	A		R	O	C	K	O	F	A	G	E	S
O	N	E	R		D	O	R	A		A	L	A	R	M
M	E	S	S		A	M	Y	S		T	E	R	S	E

WORDS FOUND INSIDE "INFORMATION" (PAGE 92)

ANSWER 1:
WHAT IS (A) RAFT?
ANSWER 2:
WHAT IS (AN) ANT?
ANSWER 3:
WHAT IS ONTARIO?
ANSWER 4:
WHAT IS MOTION?
ANSWER 5:
WHAT IS FAINT?

LANDMARKS (PAGE 94)

ANSWER 1:
WHAT IS YELLOWSTONE (NATIONAL PARK)?
ANSWER 2:
WHAT IS SPAIN?
ANSWER 3:
WHAT IS EASTER ISLAND?
ANSWER 4:
WHO IS PROMETHEUS?
ANSWER 5:
WHAT IS (THE) U.S.S. ARIZONA?

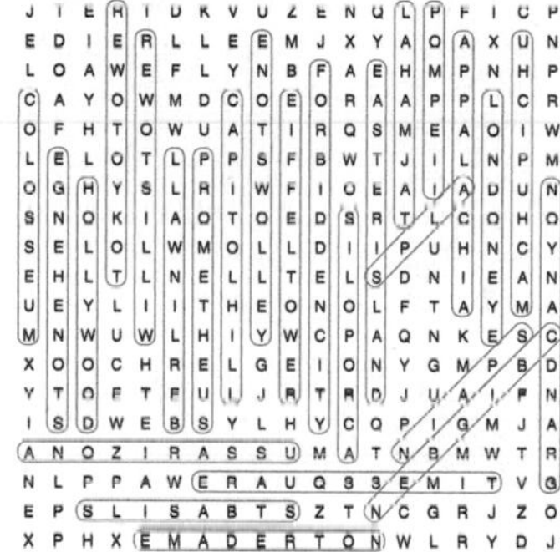

ANSWER KEY

CLASSIC POP LYRICS (PAGE 96)

ANSWER 1:
WHO IS "JUDE"? (50 ACROSS)
ANSWER 2:
WHAT IS "SURF CITY"? (47 ACROSS)
ANSWER 3:
WHAT IS "ROCK AND ROLL"? (17 ACROSS)
ANSWER 4:
WHO IS "MRS. ROBINSON"? (58 ACROSS)
ANSWER 5:
WHAT IS "JAILHOUSE ROCK"? (36 ACROSS)

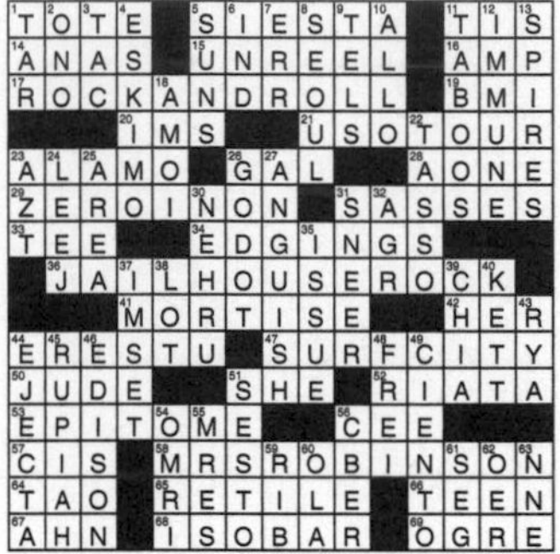

NATIONAL PARKS A–Z (PAGE 98)

ANSWER 1:
WHAT IS ARCHES?
ANSWER 2:
WHAT IS BADLANDS?
ANSWER 3:
WHAT IS GRAND CANYON?
ANSWER 4:
WHAT IS SEQUOIA?
ANSWER 5:
WHAT IS ZION?

ANCIENT EMPIRES (PAGE 100)

ANSWER 1:
WHO ARE (THE) AZTEC?
ANSWER 2:
WHO IS NERO?
ANSWER 3:
WHO IS ATTILA?
ANSWER 4:
WHO IS GENGHIS KHAN?
ANSWER 5:
WHAT IS ANATOLIA?

ANSWER KEY

COOKING "P"s (PAGE 102)

ANSWER 1:
WHAT IS PENNE? (22 ACROSS)
ANSWER 2:
WHAT IS POI? (46 DOWN)
ANSWER 3:
WHAT IS (TO) PARBOIL? (52 ACROSS)
ANSWER 4:
WHAT IS POLENTA? (20 ACROSS)
ANSWER 5:
WHAT IS PHO? (22 DOWN)

PLANES, TRAINS, AND AUTOMOBILES (PAGE 104)

ANSWER 1:
WHAT IS (THE) READING?
ANSWER 2:
WHAT IS ROLLS-ROYCE?
ANSWER 3:
WHAT IS (THE) CONCORDE?
ANSWER 4:
WHAT IS (A) DINING CAR?
ANSWER 5:
WHAT IS MCDONNELL?

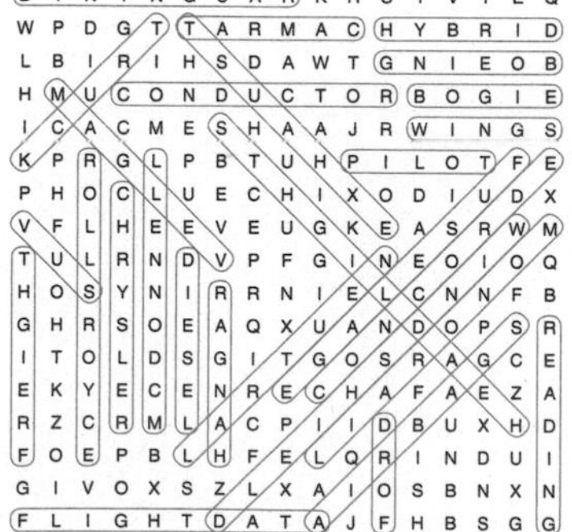

FAMOUS AMERICANS (PAGE 106)

ANSWER 1:
WHO IS NEIL ARMSTRONG? (23 ACROSS)
ANSWER 2:
WHO IS COLIN POWELL? (17 ACROSS)
ANSWER 3:
WHO IS HARRY HOUDINI? (29 ACROSS)
ANSWER 4:
WHO IS AMELIA EARHART? (47 ACROSS)
ANSWER 5:
WHO IS ABNER DOUBLEDAY? (37 ACROSS)

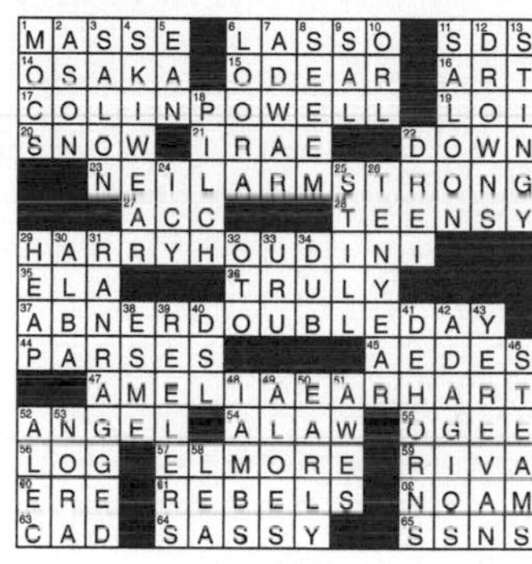

ANSWER KEY

POP MUSIC RHYME TIME (PAGE 108)

ANSWER 1:
WHAT ARE SNOOP'S COOPS?
ANSWER 2:
WHAT ARE MICK'S BICS?
ANSWER 3:
WHAT ARE SAMMY'S JAMMIES?
ANSWER 4:
WHAT ARE BOB'S LOBS?
ANSWER 5:
WHAT ARE OZZY'S FOZZIES?

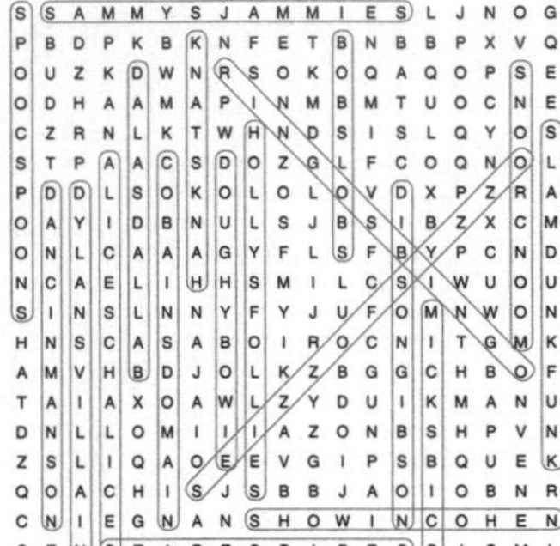

MUSEUMS (PAGE 110)

ANSWER 1:
WHO IS ANNE FRANK? (17 ACROSS)
ANSWER 2:
WHAT IS HARVARD? (56 ACROSS)
ANSWER 3:
WHAT IS LONDON? (48 DOWN)
ANSWER 4:
WHAT IS DESIGN? (11 DOWN)
ANSWER 5:
WHO IS ISAK DINESEN? (38 ACROSS)

PULITZER PRIZE WINNERS (PAGE 112)

ANSWER 1:
WHO IS FRANK MCCOURT?
ANSWER 2:
WHO IS WILLA CATHER?
ANSWER 3:
WHO IS AARON COPLAND?
ANSWER 4:
WHO IS ROBERT FROST?
ANSWER 5:
WHO IS DAVID MAMET?

F R A N K M C C R O U R T E W A B
A A R O N C O P L A N D S K H T R
A N N I E P R O U L X X D I T S D
T I S N I K A E O Z V H O D O O L
N I W R E M S W O J N X U P R R D
J C A R L S A N D B U R G U P F A
U N D O N N A T A R T T W N I T N
N R B E N G O Z H Z F H R H L R F
O T E M A M D I V A D T I O I E A
T R E L L I M N O S A J G J H B G
D P E T E R T A Y L O R H U P O I
I Y J A U W I L L A C A T H E R N
A R E K A B E I N N A I Y U M X P
Z J T R J N O S I R R O M I N O T
C O R M A C M C C A R T H Y L K B
P T L Z O S S U R D R A H C I R V
J L A R R Y M C M U R T Y I W N K

ANSWER KEY

O CANADA (PAGE 114)

ANSWER 1:
WHAT IS TORONTO? (20 ACROSS)
ANSWER 2:
WHAT IS (THE) BEAVER? (47 ACROSS)
ANSWER 3:
WHAT IS QUEBEC? (25 ACROSS)
ANSWER 4:
WHAT IS DOMINION? (37 DOWN)
ANSWER 5:
WHAT IS MANITOBA? (28 ACROSS)

SCRAMBLED SPORTS (PAGE 116)

ANSWER 1:
WHAT IS ARCHERY?
ANSWER 2:
WHAT IS BASKETBALL?
ANSWER 3:
WHAT IS GYMNASTICS?
ANSWER 4:
WHAT IS WRESTLING?
ANSWER 5:
WHAT IS SNOWBOARDING?

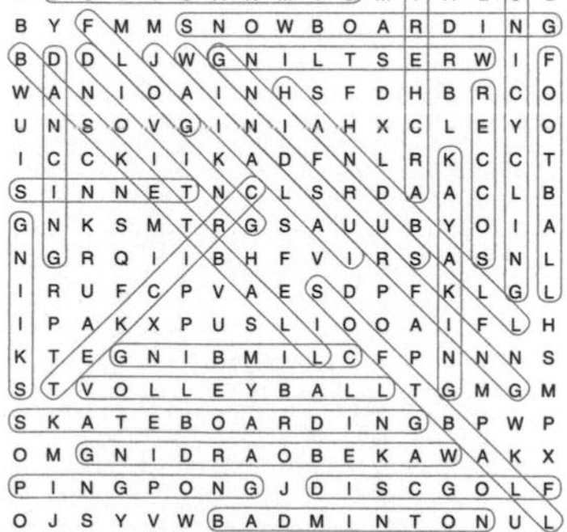

ANSWER KEY

THANKS FOR THE MEMOIRS (PAGE 118)

ANSWER 1:
WHO IS STEPHEN KING?
ANSWER 2:
WHAT IS COLOMBIA?
ANSWER 3:
WHAT IS "EAT, PRAY, LOVE"?
ANSWER 4:
WHO IS DAVID SEDARIS?
ANSWER 5:
WHO IS NELSON MANDELA?

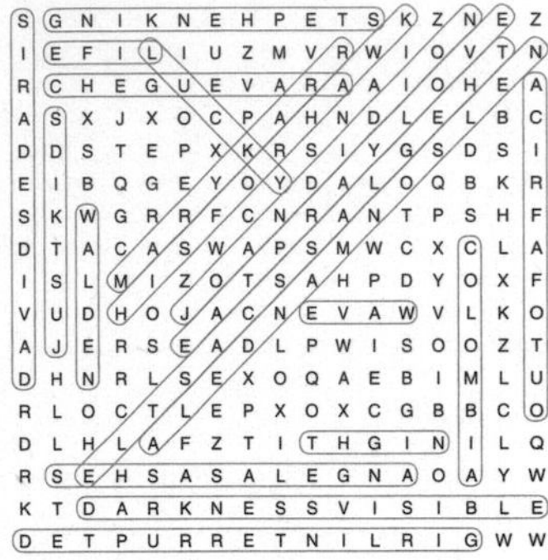

TELEVISION (PAGE 120)

ANSWER 1:
WHAT IS "GREY'S ANATOMY"? (27 ACROSS)
ANSWER 2:
WHAT IS "THE OFFICE"? (18 ACROSS)
ANSWER 3:
WHAT IS HOMELAND? (26 DOWN)
ANSWER 4:
WHAT IS "DOCTOR WHO"? (55 ACROSS)
ANSWER 5:
WHAT IS "TMZ"? (52 ACROSS)

M	A	I	D	S		S	W	A	G		O	O	N	A
A	D	I	E	U		A	A	R	P		F	L	A	M
R	E	I	G	N		T	H	E	O	F	F	I	C	E
S	S	I		R	E	E	L			O	D	O	R	S
			H	I	T	E		P	H	R	A	S	E	S
G	R	E	Y	S	A	N	A	T	O	M	Y			
N	U	T	M	E	G		S	U	M	S		T	D	S
A	S	O	N		E	R	N	I	E		L	I	R	A
T	E	N		E	R	I	E		L	S	E	V	E	N
			I	C	E	C	R	E	A	M	S	O	D	A
O	M	I	G	O	S	H		U	N	O	S			
D	O	N	E	N			O	R	D	O		T	M	Z
D	O	C	T	O	R	W	H	O		T	A	H	O	E
E	S	A	I		C	R	O	P		H	A	U	T	E
R	E	S	T		A	S	H	E		S	A	G	E	S

ANSWER KEY

THEATER (PAGE 122)

ANSWER 1:
WHAT IS "LES MISERABLES"?
ANSWER 2:
WHAT IS "RENT"?
ANSWER 3:
WHO IS ELIZA DOOLITTLE?
ANSWER 4:
WHO IS EDWIN DROOD?
ANSWER 5:
WHO IS MATTHEW SHEPARD?

VIVA MEXICO! (PAGE 124)

ANSWER 1:
WHAT IS SPAIN?
ANSWER 2:
WHO IS VICENTE FOX?
ANSWER 3:
WHAT IS GREEN?
ANSWER 4:
WHAT IS CINCO DE MAYO?
ANSWER 5:
WHO IS MAXIMILIAN?

ANSWER KEY

THE BODY HUMAN (PAGE 126)

ANSWER 1:
WHAT IS (A) MUSCLE? (44 DOWN)
ANSWER 2:
WHAT IS ENAMEL? (58 ACROSS)
ANSWER 3:
WHAT IS (THE) SMALL INTESTINE? (19 ACROSS)
ANSWER 4:
WHAT ARE (THE) CANINES? (42 DOWN)
ANSWER 5:
WHAT IS (THE) EPIGLOTTIS? (32 ACROSS)

WOMEN IN HISTORY (PAGE 128)

ANSWER 1:
WHO IS ANNE SULLIVAN?
ANSWER 2:
WHO IS SUSAN B. ANTHONY?
ANSWER 3:
WHO IS MARY TUDOR?
ANSWER 4:
WHO IS EVA PERON?
ANSWER 5:
WHO IS MARIAN ANDERSON?

ANSWER KEY

WORD ORIGINS (PAGE 130)

ANSWER 1:
WHAT IS CATARACT?
ANSWER 2:
WHAT IS CONTINENT?
ANSWER 3:
WHAT IS PROTAGONIST?
ANSWER 4:
WHAT IS (A) BANQUET?
ANSWER 5:
WHAT IS (A) SPINNAKER?

U.S. CITIES (PAGE 132)

ANSWER 1:
WHAT IS HONOLULU? (10 DOWN)
ANSWER 2:
WHAT IS BOSTON? (42 ACROSS)
ANSWER 3:
WHAT IS PHILADELPHIA? (53 ACROSS)
ANSWER 4:
WHAT IS NEW ORLEANS? (17 ACROSS)
ANSWER 5:
WHAT IS MEMPHIS? (51 ACROSS)

A	T	L	A	S	■	E	R	L	E	■	H	A	N	A
I	R	A	T	E	■	M	E	E	T	■	O	D	E	S
N	E	W	O	R	L	E	A	N	S	■	N	O	C	K
T	E	N	N	■	E	R	I	N	■	D	O	L	C	E
■	■	■	C	A	N	A	R	Y	Y	E	L	L	O	W
G	O	N	E	R	I	L	■	S	A	B	U	■	■	■
R	T	E	■	E	N	D	S	■	S	T	L	U	K	E
A	T	O	P	■	■	S	I	C	■	■	U	T	E	S
B	O	S	T	O	N	■	D	A	L	E	■	A	P	T
■	■	■	O	B	E	Y	■	M	E	M	P	H	I	S
P	H	I	L	A	D	E	L	P	H	I	A	■	■	■
R	A	V	E	N	■	S	O	F	A	■	S	A	C	K
A	D	A	M	■	A	S	P	I	R	A	T	I	O	N
D	E	N	Y	■	P	E	E	R	■	R	O	N	E	E
A	S	T	I	■	E	S	S	E	■	C	R	U	D	E

ANSWER KEY

WEIGHTS & MEASURES (PAGE 134)

ANSWER 1:
WHAT IS FATHOM? (36 DOWN)
ANSWER 2:
WHAT IS (A) BARREL? (54 ACROSS)
ANSWER 3:
WHAT IS (A) FURLONG? (37 ACROSS)
ANSWER 4:
WHAT IS (A) REAM? (10 ACROSS)
ANSWER 5:
WHAT IS (A) STONE? (1 ACROSS)

WORLD RELIGIONS (PAGE 136)

ANSWER 1:
WHAT IS ISLAM?
ANSWER 2:
WHAT IS SHINTO?
ANSWER 3:
WHAT IS HINDUISM?
ANSWER 4:
WHAT IS RASTAFARIANISM?
ANSWER 5:
WHAT IS BAHAI?

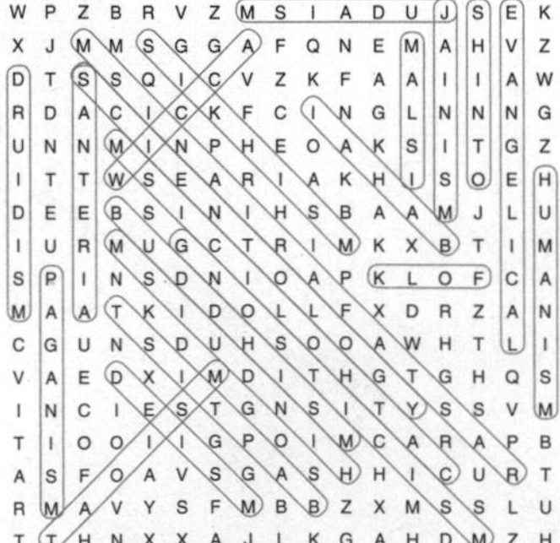